Adhd Toolkit

The Ultimate Blueprint

For Women

7 Breakthrough Strategies for ADHD Management, Success Techniques, Improve Daily Life and Transform Your Life with Proven Solutions..

Adhd Toolkit for Women (The Ultimate Step by Step Blueprint)

FREE GIFT

As a way of saying thanks for your purchase, I'm offering the book Shadow Work Journal: A Journey of Self-Discovery for FREE to my readers.

To get instant access just go to:

Inside the book, you will discover:

- How to uncover hidden aspects of yourself through guided prompts

- Techniques for integrating your shadow self into your conscious life

- Exercises to foster emotional growth and self-awareness

- Practical tips for creating a balanced and fulfilling life

If you want to embark on a journey of self-discovery and transformation, make sure to grab the free book.

Table of Contents

This is for all the women who have ever felt confused, overloaded, or too small. May you find genius in your own unique journey and thrive without shame. You're not by yourself, and you're enough.

<u>Rebecca Elwin</u>

WHY DID I WRITE THIS BOOK AND WHAT CAN YOU EXPECT FROM IT?

| **"Holding a secret story is the worst ache." From Maya Angelou**

The process of writing this book was very personal and changed me in big ways. As a woman with ADHD, I understand the challenges, grievances, and triumphs that accompany navigating life through a frequently misinterpreted perspective. I struggled with thoughts of not being competent enough, disorganization, and stress for many years. Despite my determination to succeed, I frequently found myself mired in self-doubt, unable to understand why some tasks appeared insurmountable while others were straightforward.

When I learned I wasn't broken, but just wired differently, that's when things changed for me. After coming to this realization, I embarked on a mission to redefine the experience of living with ADHD, particularly for women. I aim to transform the narrative from feelings of shame and anger to ones of strength and determination. That's why I wrote this book: to give women like you the methods, tools, and changes in thinking you need to do well in every part of your life.

AD/HD: A Different Path for Women

As different as the women who live with ADHD are, so are their experiences. Traditionally, people associate ADHD with restless boys, but women with ADHD often go unnoticed and unidentified for years. We struggle to meet social standards because of this oversight, and we often blame ourselves for problems that are out of our control. Changes in hormones, being sensitive to emotions, and having to do a lot of things at once make our journey with ADHD very difficult, but also very fulfilling when we learn to accept it.

I wanted to write a book that acknowledged these challenges. Many self-help books about ADHD don't go into enough detail about how to live as a woman with the condition. Instead, they focus on general answers that work for everyone. We intended this book to be akin to a pleasant conversation with a friend who truly understands—someone you can reach out to when you're experiencing sadness or require assistance.

What This Book Has

This book aims to assist you in comprehending ADHD, managing it, and ultimately thriving in its presence. Every part is full of useful advice for women, based on study and filled with personal stories that readers can relate to. Here's what you can expect:

Understanding gives people power.

Understanding ADHD as a unique, not a weakness, is the first step towards managing it effectively. In Chapter 1, we look at the unique brain traits of girls with ADHD, bust some myths, and learn how to see ADHD as a strength. After understanding how your brain works, you can use its amazing abilities.

There are solutions that you can use in real life.

People with ADHD may find daily tasks challenging, but it doesn't mean they can't accomplish them. Chapter 2 is full of easy-to-use tips that will help you clear your mind, make habits that last, and set up systems that work for you. These solutions are adaptable, grounded in reality, and tailored specifically for women.

Getting closer to each other

When it comes to women with ADHD, relationships can be both enjoyable and hard. In Chapter 3, you'll learn how to communicate, get along with others, and make and keep important relationships. This chapter gives you ways to improve your relationships and feel less alone, whether you're dealing with a love relationship, a friendship, or being a parent.

Getting along at work and school

For many women with ADHD, problems at work and in school are different from those for men. Chapter 4 discusses finding a job that fits your skills, avoiding distractions, and using technology to stay on track. You'll also learn ways to study and improve your skills that are easier to handle and more fun.

Making changes in your life

Chapter 5 is about the bigger picture: boosting your confidence, putting yourself first, and making your life feel like it fits with your values. You'll learn how to keep your mental and physical health in balance and build a set of tools that will help you get through the ups and downs of life.

How to Succeed with ADHD

In the last part, I talk about seven ground-breaking ways to deal with ADHD and make your life better. These proven methods are based on research, personal experience, and other women who have gone through the same. These methods are user-friendly, effective, and designed to support your long-term success.

Who This Book Is For

Read this book if you're a woman who has ever felt like the world was moving faster than her. It's for the workaholic who is trying to keep everything together, the creative person who can't seem to concentrate, and the mom who is too busy to do everything. Whether you recently received a diagnosis or have been managing ADHD for years, this book contains information and tips to help you thrive.

Women who may not be aware of having ADHD but can relate to the issues discussed here are also the target audience. A lot of women don't find out they have ADHD until they are adults, and that can change their whole lives. This book might give you the focus and tools you need if you've ever felt like you were living in chaos or were always trying to catch up.

Why do I believe in these plans?

These tips aren't just theories; real women with ADHD, including myself, have used them and found them to work. I've spent years reading, trying things out, and learning from both my own and other people's experiences. These techniques have helped me get my focus back, boost my confidence, and make my life feel real and full.

Taking care of ADHD is a process, not a goal, so I can't offer success. But I promise progress. This book has tools that will help you make changes that matter, one step at a time. If you want to make a morning routine that works for you, talk about your needs more clearly, or find peace in your job, these tips can help.

One last word

I wrote this book out of love because I want to give women with ADHD the tools they need to live their best lives. I think that you can get through tough times, focus on your skills, and reach your objectives. Having ADHD doesn't limit your abilities.

I hope that as you read these pages, you find the ideas, direction, and support you need to take charge of your journey. Do not forget that you are not the only one going through this. We can change the story about ADHD and create a world where every woman with it feels seen, supported, and powerful.

So, get a cup of tea and find a comfortable place to sit. Let's start this journey that will change our lives together. Trust yourself, and I'll support you throughout.

Welcome to Embracing Your Unique Journey with ADHD.

"Your problems do not make you who you are. You are the stronger one than them."

People with ADHD often feel like they are always fighting to stay organized, focused, and in charge. Would you believe me if I told you that ADHD is not only a problem but also a huge opportunity? What if you changed how you think about it? Instead of viewing it as a problem, consider it as a way your brain functions, providing you with imagination, energy, and new perspectives on the world.

That's what this book is all about: helping you see your ADHD not as a flaw but as a power that's just ready to be used.

Why this trip is important

I know what it's like because I have ADHD myself. It's been crazy, weird, and frustrating. Sometimes I felt hurt when people didn't understand me and told me to "just try harder" or "calm down and focus." Juggling a lot of things at once while fighting a brain that won't cooperate has made me feel overwhelmed. A lot of women have asked me why it seems like daily life is so much harder for me than it is for everyone else.

I learned something crucial along the way, though: ADHD doesn't define me. There are positive things about that part of me that people don't always notice. Everything started to change for the better once I learned how to use my brain instead of against it.

This book is my way of sharing what I have discovered with you.

The unique problems girls and women with ADHD face

It's a fact: ADHD looks different in girls and adults. People usually think of energetic kids who bounce off the walls when they hear the word "ADHD." But for many women, the symptoms are much more subtle and tiring. Forgetting things, being late all the time, being emotionally sensitive, and having a strong sense of being confused are all signs of ADHD.

We're very good at hiding the chaos and putting on a brave face while fighting feelings of not being good enough behind closed doors. As women, we've learned to hide our problems because we're supposed to do it all: run the home, do well at work, take care of our relationships, and still find time for self-care.

It costs something to hide, though. It makes us feel alone and unnoticed, like we're failing at something that everyone else does so well.

We wrote this book to reassure you that you're not failing. You can handle life with a brain that works differently, and that's fine. Because you're not alone, you don't have to act like someone else to succeed.

Thinking of ADHD as a Superpower

ADHD is a way of life, not just a set of symptoms. While ADHD certainly presents challenges, it also possesses remarkable abilities. A lot of the time, women with ADHD are artistic, sensitive, caring, and strong. We see links that other people miss. We care about things with a lot of heart and energy.

If you want to do well with ADHD, don't try to "fix" yourself. Instead, learn how to work with your brain rather than against it. It's about focusing on your skills and getting help for the things you find hard.

This book is practical, inspiring, and specifically designed for women like you, offering a wealth of tips and recommendations. Managing your daily tasks, making deep connections with other people, doing outstanding work, and changing the way you think are all parts of this journey that are meant to help you reach your full potential.

How Important Are Little Wins?

Learning that change doesn't happen overnight is something I've learned on this road. It's not about making big changes or trying to be perfect. It involves taking small, manageable steps that, over time, add up to significant progress.

Instead of changing everything about your life, you could start by adding one new habit that makes getting ready in the morning easier. You could also use just one method to stay focused at work. All of these little wins add up and have an effect on every part of your life.

This book is filled with small steps that you can implement immediately. I want to give you tools you can use right away to feel more confident, organized, and in control.

A safe place to grow

You should feel safe reading this book. You should be free to openly discuss your issues without fear of judgment. Too often, women with ADHD get too much help that doesn't make sense or is too much to handle. People often advise us to "just get organized" or "try harder," as though we haven't already exerted our utmost effort.

You won't find that here. Do not force yourself into a mold that doesn't suit you. It means coming up with plans that respect you for who you are.

We will not shame people, set unrealistic standards, or provide one-size-fits-all answers. Instead, you'll find support, understanding, and useful tips that are specific to your trip.

What You Should Expect

What does it mean to live with and manage ADHD as a woman? That's what the next few parts will be all about. Check out what's in store:

Learning About Your ADHD Brain: We'll look at how ADHD affects women differently and find the strengths that are hiding below the surface.

Surviving in Everyday Life: You'll learn useful ways to handle tasks, clear your mind, and form habits that last.

Making Connections That Matter: Learn how to tell people what you need, keep relationships strong, and build a group that helps each other.

How to Do Well at Work and School: You'll find tools to help you do well in both work and academic settings, such as job tips and learning hacks.

Changing Your Life: We'll work on building your confidence, putting yourself first, and making your life feel real and complete.

The ADHD Success Blueprint gives you access to seven groundbreaking ways to deal with ADHD and reach your goals.

A trip that's worth taking

I'm not going to say this trip is going to be easy. There will be days when the chaos is too much, other things get in the way, or you don't think you can progress. But I promise that every move you make will be worth it.

This book isn't about being great; it's about getting better. It means giving yourself the freedom to let go of guilt and follow your own path. It's about being content with small wins and enjoying every moment of growth.

I hope that reading these pages gives you a sense of strength and reminds you that you are strong, capable, and deserve to succeed. Your ADHD doesn't diminish you or limit your abilities.

Allow us to begin.

For now, take a deep breath and know that you're where you should be. Now is your chance to learn, grow, and discover. You've come to the right place if you want to find answers to your everyday problems or learn more about yourself.

You're not going through this by yourself. We will find tools, methods, and mindset changes to help you manage and live with ADHD.

Let's see the brilliant side of your ADHD and help you reach your full potential. Now is the time to make your life better. Allow us to begin!

CHAPTER 1: UNLOCKING THE ADHD ADVANTAGE

"Your ADHD isn't a limitation—it's an untapped reservoir of potential waiting to be unleashed."

SEEING ADHD AS A STRENGTH: YOUR ADHD, YOUR SUPERPOWER

"What if your ADHD wasn't something you had to fix but something you should be proud of?"

We need to tell a new story about ADHD, one based on facts, real-life examples, and hope. For many years, people have viewed ADHD as a disease, a weakness, or a problem that requires fixing. But new studies and the opinions of well-known experts are calling that old view into question. Experts are increasingly understanding the creative, flexible, and strong wiring of people with ADHD.

Dr. Edward Hallowell, a famous ADHD expert and author of Driven to Distraction, says, "Our differences are our greatest strengths." Hallowell says that people with ADHD have "extraordinary potential to innovate, lead, and connect," but only if they know how to use their special energy.

We're going to talk about how you can use your ADHD for beneficial purposes by seeing it as a gift.

Why people often get ADHD wrong

Attention, focus, and order have been big parts of the story about ADHD for a long time. People like teachers, bosses, and even family members who mean well may only talk about the problems without ever noticing the strengths.

However, having ADHD does not necessarily mean that your brain is malfunctioning. This implies that your brain functions differently. While neurotypical brains typically follow a linear path, ADHD brains exhibit a flurry of ideas, connections, and energy. The challenging part is not stopping these bursts; the challenging part is learning how to aim them well.

One example is how easy it is for your mind to get excited when you're working on something you really care about. This phenomenon, known as "hyperfocus," is unique to individuals with ADHD. It means putting a lot of effort into things that interest you and coming up with creative, new, and amazing results.

Hyperfocus, on the other hand, doesn't always come with a guide. That's why it's important to learn how to direct your brain toward what's most important.

How to Turn Problems Into Strengths

This may make you wonder, "If ADHD is a superpower, then why does it feel so hard sometimes?"Finding the right mix between your skills and ways to deal with problems is the key.

Another well-known expert on ADHD, Dr. Russell Barkley, says that people with ADHD have a brain that works on an "interest-based nervous system." This means that they do best when tasks are stimulating and important, but struggle when they are routine or dull.

You shouldn't see this as a problem but as a tool. Your brain is always looking for things that make you content and motivated. The important thing is to figure out what makes you fulfilled and make sure that more of those things happen in your daily life.

Use a real-life case. Maria, a graphic artist with ADHD, frequently lost her temper because she struggled to maintain order. She had a lot to do and never seemed to get it done. But when she changed the way she thought about things, she saw that her ADHD was a gift: it let her think visually and solve problems in ways that her peers couldn't. Maria changed the way she worked and started doing well in her job by playing to her skills and using tools like visual project boards.

You can do the same thing. The first step is to ask yourself, "What am I naturally good at?"There is hope for many women with ADHD because they are creative, caring, and able to see things from different points of view.

How Strengths Can Help People with ADHD

This is backed up by science. Studies are increasingly demonstrating that individuals with ADHD excel in scenarios that necessitate innovative thinking. The Gift of Adult ADHD author Dr. Lara Honos-Webb says that people with ADHD are often innovators, problem-solvers, and change-makers. "ADHD is not a disorder of attention," she says. It's an intriguing disease. When you apply your skills, you are unstoppable.

One intriguing example of this is how people with ADHD deal with new things. Your brain's innate desire for excitement naturally draws you to problems that require quick thinking and flexibility. This explains why you excel in challenging situations where others struggle.

Don't fight your need for excitement; instead, figure out how to use it to your advantage. For instance, if you find yourself getting bored with mundane tasks like paying your bills, consider engaging in these tasks while listening to your favorite music or turning them into a timed challenge. You're not "lazy" or "unmotivated." Your brain just needs fun and rewards.

Tips on How to Start Reframing ADHD

Thinking differently about ADHD is the first step to managing it. How you talk to yourself about your brain needs to change. How to start:

Take note of your wins:

Think about the times your ADHD helped you. You may have figured out a problem at work that no one else could. Your understanding may have helped a friend get through a rough patch. Note these times down. Have fun with them.

Focus on what you love:

What gets you excited? Do the things that make you happy, whether they're art, science, teaching, or starting your own business. Passion is beneficial for your ADHD brain, and doing what you love can help you reach your full potential.

Utilize the resources that will assist you.

Changing how you think about ADHD doesn't mean ignoring your problems. It means coming up with plans that work for your brain. Set timers and visual aids to help you remember to do things. Also, make systems that work for you.

Get help from other people:

You're not by yourself. You can find groups of women with ADHD who can help you along the way. Connecting with other people, whether it's through an online group, a neighborhood meetup, or a trusted friend, can be very helpful.

A strength, not a weakness.

You may still be unsure. The world isn't always kind to people who don't agree with you, after all. However, there are numerous historical examples of individuals who have utilized their ADHD as a strength. People with ADHD who have been successful, like Richard Branson and Michael Phelps, have talked about it in public.

It's possible for you to write your own story. Dealing with ADHD isn't easy, but it's important to see the whole picture, including the difficulties and the gifts.

When you view your ADHD as a positive trait, you begin to transform your behavior in the world. You stop being sorry for being yourself and start building on your strengths.

The Way Forward

After this, where do you go? Start out small. Find one area where your ADHD has helped you start well. Perhaps it's your ability to think creatively, demonstrate empathy, or solve problems effectively. Don't forget to read it every time you start to question yourself. Write it down and keep it close.

After that, do the next thing. Pick one technique from this book and use it daily. Make a promise to try something new, whether it's using technology to stay on track or setting up a habit loop based on rewards.

It's not about being perfect on this road; it's about making progress. It's about finding what works and being proud of your ADHD brain's intelligence.

Remember, your ADHD is not a weakness, but a hidden strength. The world needs your special thoughts, energy, and point of view. Okay, let's begin. Your ability is ready for you.

Understanding the Brain of a Woman with ADHD: What Is Different About ADHD in Women?

"It's not that women with ADHD aren't heard; it's that for too long, people have had the wrong idea about them."

For a long time, people believed that ADHD primarily affected restless boys who caused problems in the classroom. Due to this outdated belief, many women struggled alone, questioning why life felt so difficult. But the study is changing the story. Scientists and other experts are now shedding light on the unique ways that ADHD shows up in women. The results are both reassuring and powerful.

Let's talk about what makes the brains of women with ADHD so different and how knowing these differences can help you reach your full potential.

What Women Go Through: Why They Are Often Ignored

It's not uncommon to feel like no one notices or accepts ADHD. "Girls and women with ADHD often develop strong coping mechanisms to hide their symptoms, making them less noticeable to teachers, parents, and even healthcare providers," says Dr. Patricia Quinn, a leader in ADHD research for women.

Boys with ADHD often act out their symptoms by being reckless or restless, but girls with ADHD tend to keep them to themselves. Instead of being called "too loud" or "too active," women with ADHD might be called careless, emotional, or daydreamers. Many women don't get help for this silent battle until they are adults, often after years of being frustrated at themselves and blaming themselves.

Someone may have told you that you're "too sensitive" or that you need to "focus harder." These rude comments can hurt, but they also show that people have a serious misunderstanding of what it's like to have ADHD as a woman.

What hormones do to the brains of girls with ADHD?

Among the most notable differences between men and women with ADHD is hormones. In contrast to men, whose hormone levels stay mostly steady throughout their lives, women's hormone levels change a lot, especially during menstruation, pregnancy, and menopause.

"Hormonal changes have a profound effect on ADHD symptoms," says Dr. Ellen Littman, a counselor who specializes in ADHD in women. Dopamine production is already low in people with ADHD, but estrogen raises it. Symptoms can get a lot worse when estrogen levels drop.

Sometimes, times of your cycle might make your ADHD easier to handle, but during PMS or after giving birth, it might become too much for you to handle. It's not your fantasy; it's science. Changes in hormones can make symptoms worse, like confusion, emotional sensitivity, and trouble focusing.

With this information, you can start to see trends in your symptoms and make plans based on those patterns. If the week before your period is especially hard, you might want to do fewer difficult chores or prioritize yourself.

Emotional sensitivity is like a sword with two edges.

Another trait of women with ADHD is their emotional awareness. It can be challenging to deal with this, but it's also a strength. A lot of the time, women with ADHD are very intuitive, socially aware, and empathic.

However, emotional sensitivity can exacerbate negative emotions such as rejection, criticism, or conflict. This is what ADHD expert Dr. William Dodson calls "rejection sensitivity dysphoria" (RSD), and it happens a lot to people with ADHD. He says, "RSD isn't just being sad; it's a strong emotional reaction to feeling rejected or unsuccessful."

You're not the only one who has ever thought about a talk over and over and wondered if they said the wrong thing or who has been hurt by a small criticism. The positive news is that knowing this part of your ADHD can help you come up with ways to handle it.

For instance, when you feel rejected or criticized, tell yourself that your feelings are real but not always true. What seems like an attack on your person could just be a harmless comment. You can also deal with strong feelings in a healthy way by doing exercises that help you ground yourself, writing in a book, or talking to a friend you trust.

Too much mental load and multitasking.

Have you ever experienced a sense of your mind operating at high speed, managing numerous tasks, responsibilities, and concerns? Women with ADHD frequently experience overwhelming thoughts due to their responsibilities as parents, lovers, workers, and others.

According to Doctor Ned Hallowell, women with ADHD often face challenges: they must navigate a world that demands linear thinking while managing a brain that craves spontaneity and creativity.

As a result? Tiredness.

However, being able to multitask is not a sign of worth, and saying no is fine. Focus on putting what really counts first instead of trying to do everything at once. Get everything out of your head and on paper with a "brain dump" or other similar tool. Then, choose the three most important things you need to do first. This small change can help you get back in charge and feel less overwhelmed.

Why It's Important to Know How Your Brain Works

It's not just fascinating to learn how ADHD affects women in particular; it's life-changing. Once you understand why your brain works the way it does, you won't blame yourself for problems that aren't your fault.

Imagine that you were driving a car with a stick shift and didn't know how to use it. You'd keep stalling out and getting angry. But it's easier and smoother to drive once you know how the gears work. Your ADHD brain operates similarly.

How can you make your brain work for you?

Write down your symptoms:

Pay attention to how your ADHD symptoms change over time, especially when your hormones are changing. In a book or an app, write down when you feel most focused and when you feel most stressed. You'll start to see patterns over time that will help you make better plans.

Draw on your emotional strengths:

Being sensitive is a gift because it lets you connect deeply with others and handle relationships with understanding. With this strength, you can make friends and surround yourself with people who understand and support you.

Adapt systems to assist individuals with ADHD.

It's okay if traditional ways of organizing don't work for you. Try different tools, such as color-coded maps, visual prompts, and timers, to see what works best for your brain.

Learn to be kind to yourself:

Keep in mind that ADHD is not a flaw; it's a way of thinking. When things don't go as planned, be kind to yourself and enjoy your wins, no matter how small.

You're not alone.

Remember that you're not on this road by yourself. There are millions of women facing the same problems and finding their own powers. In addition to managing your ADHD symptoms, you must change your story and realize that you are more than your problems.

Your mind is very smart, artistic, and can do amazing things. Let's keep working together to find its full potential.

BUSTING ADHD MYTHS: COMMON FALSE IDEAS AND THE REAL STORY

"The greatest threat to knowledge is not ignorance, but the delusion of knowledge." –
Stephen Hawking

A lot of people have the wrong idea about ADHD. They appear in everyday conversations, media, and medicine. Not only do these myths mislead, but they also create obstacles. They make you doubt your own experiences, think you're the issue, or think you're not putting in enough effort. However, the truth is that being lazy, stupid, or bad-natured does not cause ADHD. Understanding the wiring of your brain requires dispelling common misconceptions about it.

Myth 1: ADHD is just a reason to be lazy.

This can be upsetting and frustrating if someone has said you used ADHD as an excuse. ADHD is related to poor focus and brain function, not laziness. "ADHD is not a deficit of attention, but a deficit of self-regulation," says Dr. Russell Barkley, one of the most famous researchers on ADHD.

This doesn't mean you're lazy; it just means your brain has trouble setting priorities, starting tasks, and staying focused, especially when the task seems dull or too much to handle. If you're really into what you're doing, you can hyperfocus and finish hours in minutes. Do you perceive this as a sign of laziness?

Things you can do:

In the event that someone says you're lazy, tell yourself that ADHD is a brain disorder and not a character flaw. Timer systems or external responsibilities can assist you in initiating tasks. And remember that you're not failing; your brain has its own needs.

Myth 2: ADHD is only about being too active.

People often assume that ADHD always manifests as restlessness. This myth disproportionately affects women, as women often exhibit less noticeable signs of ADHD. Instead of bouncing off the walls, you might find yourself thinking, zoning out during talks, or feeling as though your mind is overflowing with thoughts.

"Women with ADHD often internalize their symptoms, leading to feelings of inadequacy and guilt because their struggles are invisible to others," says Dr. Kathleen Nadeau, an expert on women with ADHD.

People around you might not see what's wrong, but you might feel like you're always fighting an unseen war. It must be tiring, right?

Things you can do:

Start by recognizing what you've been through. There is no wrong way to have ADHD, whether it shows up as restlessness, inattention, or a mix of the two. You don't need to conform to a specific stereotype in order to receive understanding or assistance.

Myth 3: ADHD is only a problem for kids.

You've probably heard the phrase "you'll grow out of it" a lot. This myth can make you feel like a failure if you keep having problems as an adult. The facts, on the other hand, say otherwise. ADHD is a disease that lasts a lifetime, but the signs change over time.

"Adults with ADHD face challenges just as significant as those in childhood," says Dr. Edward Hallowell, one of the first people to study ADHD. "These challenges look different—often manifesting as difficulties with time management, emotional regulation, and maintaining relationships."

Have you ever had trouble remembering when things were due, felt like you were always late, or reacted too strongly to small irritations? This is simply a manifestation of your adult ADHD at work; it does not imply that you are being childish or careless.

Things you can do:

Know that ADHD isn't something you can grow out of; it's something you can grow with. Any age can succeed if you learn techniques for your stage of life.

Myth 4: ADHD Is Not Real

This is one of the most pervasive myths. Many people who say ADHD is "not real" say it's overdiagnosed, the result of negligent parenting, or just a result of living in the modern world. However, ADHD is one of the most extensively researched neurological disorders globally, with decades' worth of evidence supporting its existence.

"ADHD is as real as diabetes or asthma," says Dr. Thomas Brown, a clinical psychologist who specializes in ADHD. It is a cognitive disorder that affects the parts of the brain that control mood, memory, and attention.

People who don't believe in ADHD often don't understand it. People who don't have ADHD can't see the struggles you go through every day, so they downplay your problems.

<u>Things you can do:</u>

Learn as much as you can. Learn about the scientific facts behind ADHD and share them with others. If someone has doubts, just carefully give them information or point them in the direction of reliable sources.

Myth 5: Medicine can cure everything.

Someone once told you, "Just take your medicine, and you'll be fine." Medication can help people with ADHD a lot, but it's not a fix or an answer that works for everyone.

A well-known expert on ADHD, Dr. William Dodson, says, "Medication helps with the physical symptoms of ADHD, like impulsivity and focus, but it doesn't teach you skills or strategies for managing daily life."

Medication can't help you get your life in order, set priorities, or fix relationships that are getting tense. You can't see the whole picture with just this one piece.

<u>Things you can do:</u>

When taking medication, you should also engage in behavioral techniques, coaching, or therapy. Additionally, remember that it's perfectly acceptable to not require medication. What counts is that you find what works for you.

What These Myths Mean for You

It's not enough that these myths are false; they hurt. They make you question yourself, feel alone, and find it difficult to ask for help. They may stop you from seeking work assistance or telling loved ones you have ADHD.

Breaking these myths requires more than just correcting false information; you also need to reclaim your own narrative. "I'm not broken" is what it's about. There's nothing wrong with the way my brain works.

Getting Past the Myths

It's freeing to know the truth about ADHD. It helps you let go of shame, focus on tactics that make you stronger, and accept your abilities.

To regain control, take the following actions:

<u>Learn something:</u>

Read books, listen to podcasts, or join online groups that talk about ADHD in women. You will be better able to fight misunderstandings if you understand more.

<u>Put Limits On It:</u>

Do not feel like you have to give anyone a reason for your ADHD. Make sure your words are true if you share.

<u>Find Your Group:</u>

Get together with people who understand, such as in an online chat, a support group, or with a friend who also has ADHD. It can make all the difference to know you're not alone.

A Different View

While ADHD is real, complex, and poorly understood, it is manageable. In order for people to understand, grow, and feel empowered, we need to bust more myths.

Take a deep breath and remind yourself that you know the truth the next time someone says that your ADHD is an excuse or that it's not real. You're not lazy. You're not hurt. You're unique, and that's strong.

Let's change the story about ADHD one truth at a time.

ADHD AT EVERY STAGE OF LIFE: HOW IT CHANGES OVER TIME

"ADHD is in your whole story and changes and grows as you go through each stage."

People often associate the term "ADHD" with a child who is excessively busy and agitated in class. But the truth is that ADHD isn't just a problem for kids. Changing and adjusting as you grow is part of the process. ADHD expert Dr. Kathleen Nadeau says, "The challenges that people with ADHD face may not change, but the symptoms may stay the same as life demands change."

Let's look at how ADHD shows up and changes at different stages of life. This shows where you've been, are, and want to go.

Childhood: The Start of How We See Ourselves

People who told you as a kid that you had ADHD may have said things like, "She's just distracted" or "She's not living up to her potential." Girls with ADHD don't usually look like hyperactive boys. Instead, there is less noise, like daydreaming in class, failing to do homework, or losing focus during talks.

These experiences have the power to alter your self-perception. You may have felt like you were always failing as a child, no matter how hard you tried. Dr. Patricia Quinn, an expert on ADHD in girls, says that a lot of girls with ADHD experience "imposter syndrome" early on, where they feel like they have to fake it all the time to keep up.

It is important to know that your early problems were not your fault. You didn't have the tools or help as a child to deal with ADHD well. Take a moment to be kind to your younger self when you think about this time. With the tools she had, she was doing her best.

Teenage years: The Storm of Expectations

Teenage years are crazy for everyone, but for girls with ADHD, things often feel even worse. All of a sudden, you have to deal with the stress of school, social relationships, and additional activities while also dealing with changes in your hormones that make your ADHD symptoms worse.

This period often brings emotional awareness to the forefront. You may have cried over something you thought was unfair or felt completely crushed by a disappointing grade. This isn't a flaw; it's how ADHD affects the way your brain controls your emotions.

You may have also been smart enough to finish a project you liked, but then you couldn't focus on something boring. This is a sign of ADHD: you excel at jobs that pique your interest but struggle with everyday tasks.

<u>Things you can do:</u>

When you reflect on your teenage years, consider how the experiences you had shaped your current approach to dealing with situations. Did you learn how to hide how difficult things felt? Did you overcompensate by striving for perfection? With this knowledge, you can break harmful habits that are holding you back.

Growing up as a young adult involves balancing independence with overwhelming responsibilities.

As women with ADHD become adults, they often go through a turning point. You suddenly find yourself without the structure that school and family once provided, and you must establish your own path. At this point, many women find it difficult to avoid ADHD.

You may have had trouble keeping track of your money, meeting goals, or keeping up with relationships. You may have wondered, "Why can't I handle this like everyone else?" when things like going food shopping or paying your bills seemed too hard for you."

"Adult responsibilities require strong executive function skills, which are exactly the areas where ADHD creates challenges," says Dr. Russell Barkley. This does not imply a lack of ability; rather, it necessitates the use of brain-specific tools and methods.

If you've ever forgotten to pay a bill until it was past due, it's not because you're careless. You have trouble with time-blindness, which makes it challenging to keep track of due dates. You can fix this by using automatic methods or setting alarms.

<u>Things you can do:</u>

At this point, you should focus on making habits that work for people with ADHD. Break up big jobs into smaller ones, use visual aids, and enjoy every little bit of progress. Gaining independence is a process, not a goal.

The Balancing Act of Motherhood

Being a mother is a deep and life-changing experience, but for women with ADHD, it can also feel like they're walking into a pressure cooker. You suddenly control your own and someone else's lives.

This stage often shows how challenging it is for people with ADHD to organize, keep track of time, and control their emotions. You may forget about meetings, lose track of baby bags, or feel too busy to handle all the demands of being a parent.

But here's the truth: having ADHD also makes you a better mother. Your understanding lets you connect deeply with your child, your imagination makes boring tasks fun, and your ability to focus on one thing at a time can help you solve any problem.

As Dr. Hallowell says, "Being a parent with ADHD means accepting that your child isn't perfect." Your love and hard work are more important than the odd mess.

Things you can do:

Take care of yourself first as a mother. It's not selfish; it's important. Get help from a partner, a friend, or a doctor, and don't be afraid to give chores that feel too much to handle to other people. Remember that you are teaching your child how to be strong and flexible.

Middle-Aged Adulthood: Looking Back and Starting Over

As your kids get bigger or your job gets more stable, you may find yourself thinking back on your journey with ADHD. Middle age is often a time of recovery, a chance to focus on your skills and break out of old habits that aren't helping you.

This stage provides clarity for many women. You start to see how ADHD has changed your life, not only as a problem but also as a source of new ideas and strength. You might find yourself going back to interests you put on hold or changing your idea of what success means to you.

But changes in hormones during perimenopause and menopause can make ADHD symptoms worse. You may forget things more easily, get angry, or have trouble focusing. Being aware and seeking help can help you deal with this normal part of life.

Things you can do:

If you're at this point, be kind to yourself. Enjoy how far you've come and allow yourself to focus on what really means something to you. For hormonal changes, get help, whether it's from a doctor, by making changes to your habits, or by practicing awareness.

Wisdom and legacy in later life

ADHD doesn't disappear with age, but it becomes more isolated. A lot of women have found ways and tactics that work for them by the time they are older. You understand how to use your skills and deal with problems.

At this point, you should share what you know. You are empowered to change the story about ADHD for future generations by being an example for younger people with ADHD, raising awareness, or just living your life honestly.

Things you can do:

Think about what you want to leave behind. What aspects of yourself have changed as a result of ADHD? How can you use what you've learned to give other people strength? This is your chance to show that you know everything about your trip.

Your journey with ADHD is evolving as you progress.

ADHD changes as you do. It grows, shifts, and evolves with you. At every stage of life, there are new challenges and chances, but you are always the same. You possess strength, artistic ability, and the ability to excel at any age.

Remember that having ADHD isn't a problem; it's a part of your life that gives it color, depth, and complexity. Know that you're not alone as you go through each step. People are still telling your story, and your journey is unique.

How to Focus and Keep Your Balance: What Your Brain Really Wants

"When you understand how your ADHD brain works, you can reach your full potential."

When you have ADHD, it can be challenging to focus and keep your balance. Your mind is full of ideas one minute and blank the next. It's like trying to start a car without gas. What's going on below the surface? Not only is it fascinating to learn about the science behind your ADHD brain, it's also powerful. It gives you the knowledge and tools to work with your brain instead of against it all the time.

We'll discuss your mind, what it needs, and how to create a space for balance and attention.

What is going on inside your brain?

Discussing dopamine helps us understand ADHD. Dr. William Dodson, a renowned expert on ADHD, asserts that individuals with ADHD possess a neural system that is shaped by their interests. Important objects or goals can focus and motivate neurotypical brains. ADHD brains, on the other hand, need interest, novelty, or urgency.

Dopamine, often referred to as the "motivation molecule," plays a crucial role in this situation. People with ADHD don't have enough dopamine in their brains, which makes it harder to stay focused or finish jobs that aren't naturally interesting.

Have you ever noticed that it's difficult to start things that don't seem important when you're really into something you love, like a creative project or binge-watching your favorite show? That's how dopamine works. When your brain doesn't get the excitement it needs, it's challenging to concentrate.

Why is maintaining balance so difficult?

Balance and focus go hand in hand. When your brain has trouble keeping your attention, it makes it challenging to keep your life in balance. Your schedule becomes unmanageable, tasks continue to accumulate, and you experience a constant sense of catching up.

This is your brain telling you what it needs, not a sign of failure. You don't have to do everything perfectly to achieve balance. It involves creating processes that align with your brain's natural functioning, rather than conforming to external expectations.

For instance, standard ways of managing time don't work well for people with ADHD because they depend on strict routines and linear thinking. Instead, brains with ADHD do best when they are flexible and leave room for freedom and creativity.

Your brain needs to stay balanced and pay attention.

What does your brain really need to do well if you have ADHD? The answer rests in making sure that dopamine levels are stable, thoughts are clear, and emotions are stable. Let us take it one step at a time:

Stimulation at the Correct Amount

Your brain needs excitement, but too much can be too much for it to handle. To find the "sweet spot," you need to do things that challenge and thrill you without becoming too chaotic.

For instance, if you find it difficult to concentrate on everyday chores, try doing them while listening to music or setting a timer for a fun challenge. Your brain is more likely to pay attention when there is a sense of surprise or urgency.

Breaks to Recharge

Rest is just as important as getting things done, despite what most people think. To recover, process knowledge, and keep your emotions in check, your brain needs time to do nothing.

Your brain is like a battery. Not taking breaks means running out of energy and not being productive. Plan small, scheduled breaks throughout the day to help you get back on track.

Mind and Body Link

The way your body works has a big effect on how well your brain can focus and balance. Getting enough exercise, food, and sleep isn't just nice to have; they're necessary for managing ADHD.

Dr. Edward Hallowell talks a lot about how important exercise is and calls it "nature's Ritalin." Even a short walk can raise dopamine levels, make you feel better, and help you concentrate.

In the same way, eating foods high in protein can help keep your energy level steady, and making sleep a priority can help your brain heal and reset.

<u>Structures on the outside</u>

Brains that have ADHD work best with outside tools and cues. Tools like calendars, visible notes, and organizational apps can help you remember things like due dates and keep your desk clean.

Try making a plan for your day on a whiteboard if you find it challenging to keep up with your work. Seeing everything at once helps your brain organize and prioritize.

Answering some frequently asked questions about balance and focus

The question you may have is, "Why do I feel so disorganized even when I try to concentrate?"That is a beneficial question, and the answer lies in how ADHD affects executive function, which is the brain's capacity to organize, plan, and carry out tasks.

If you suffer from executive failure, you may understand the necessary actions but struggle to initiate them. Instead of laziness, there's a gap between your intentions and actions. Making steps that are small and simple to handle can help close this gap. Focus on one job at a time, like "I'll start by clearing the table," instead of saying, "I need to clean the whole house."

People often ask, "Why can I focus so well on some things but not others?" Your brain's wiring follows your interests. When you engage in activities that spark curiosity or excitement, your brain's dopamine system naturally activates. Boring activities do not activate your brain's dopamine system. Knowing this can help you stop judging yourself and start coming up with entertaining ways to do things you don't enjoy.

A Day in the Life of an ADHD Brain That Can Stay Numb and Focused

Imagine getting up in the morning and setting clear goals for the day. You don't start working on a long list of things right away; instead, you stick to a few important jobs and make goals that you can reach. To stay on track, you set a timer and give yourself a prize after each job.

You take short breaks during the day to recover. You stop, breathe, and start over when you feel stressed. You aim for growth instead of perfection because you know that balance doesn't mean doing everything, but doing what's most important.

It's not just a dream. It's possible if you have the right attitude and plan.

Create your own strategy to maintain focus and maintain equilibrium.

Here's a simple plan to start satisfying your brain's desires:

Morning Routine: Do something that makes you feel positive to start the day, like drinking water, exercising, or writing in a book. It establishes your goal-setting and balance.

Managing your tasks: Use tools like the Pomodoro Technique (work for 25 minutes, then take a 5-minute break) to stay focused without burning out.

Celebrate Wins: Reward yourself for every little victory, like finishing a job or taking a break when you needed one. Positive feedback raises both dopamine and drive.

After the day, consider what worked and what didn't. This helps you change and get better at what you're doing.

Your mind and your strength.

Focus and balance Science isn't about making your brain fit into a box; it's about letting your brain work the way it naturally does and making a space for it to shine.

You can still focus and keep your balance even though you have ADHD. It provides an opportunity for you to discover unique methods of thriving that suit your needs. If you know what your brain needs, you can live a life that makes you feel strong, accomplished, and calm.

Now, take a deep breath. You can do this. You have ADHD. Together, we'll use its power to make a life where balance and focus feel not only possible, but normal.

Chapter 1: How to Get the Most Out of ADHD

The most important things to remember from Chapter 1 are:

- You possess exceptional strength due to your ADHD. Individuals with ADHD possess creativity, empathy, and the ability to think innovatively. Try seeing it as a benefit instead of a flaw.
- Understanding the Female ADHD Brain: Due to the mild signs and the potential impact of hormones on the brain, women with ADHD often receive little attention. The first step to success is understanding your brain.
- Busting Myths About ADHD: Having ADHD doesn't mean you're lazy, have undesirable habits, or aren't smart. It's a difference in neurodevelopment that requires specific methods.
- ADHD at Every Stage of Life: ADHD changes as people go through life. From childhood to parenting and beyond, knowing how it changes over time helps you adapt and grow.
- The Science Behind Balance and Focus: Your brain needs fresh ideas, order, and excitement. You can find focus and balance in your daily life if you learn to meet its needs.

Now that you know ADHD and how it works, make real-life tools. The second chapter will teach you ways to clear your thoughts, make habits that last, and make your daily routine work for you. Let's jump right in!

CHAPTER 2: THRIVING IN YOUR DAILY ROUTINE

"Success doesn't come from perfection; it comes from building routines that work for you."

How to Clear Your Mind of Chaos to Focus Better: The Art of Decluttering Your Mind

"Does your mind ever feel like it has 25 tabs open at the same time?"

You want to concentrate, but your mind keeps going too fast. There are things you forgot to do, talks that keep playing over and over in your head, and fears about tomorrow. Your brain feels like it's buzzing with static. It's hard to focus when your mind is full of junk. For women with ADHD, it can feel like the chaos never ends. You're not the only one going through this, and there is a way out. Getting rid of mental clutter doesn't mean shutting down your thoughts; it means putting them in order so you can concentrate on what's important.

Why do people with ADHD have so much mental clutter?

Your brain isn't jumbled because you're careless or confused. This happens because ADHD affects your executive function, which is the part of your brain that controls your emotions, chores, and goals.

A top expert on ADHD, Dr. Thomas Brown, says that people with ADHD have trouble blocking out information that isn't important. This means that each thought, worry, and idea is trying to get your attention, making it difficult to clear your mind.

You've probably experienced this when you had to make a simple decision or couldn't begin a job because your mind was occupied with other tasks. It's not a sign of laziness or a lack of effort; your brain is simply trying to manage too much at once.

What mental clutter does to your daily life?

Mental clutter hinders concentration and affects virtually every aspect of life. There are times when it can make you forget about plans, lose track of time, or feel stuck when you have a lot to do. It may also drain your energy, making you restless and unable to get things done.

Consider the last time you attempted to relax, only to find your mind racing. This mental confusion is causing you to feel uncomfortable. It's nearly impossible to establish priorities or complete tasks effectively when your mind is overloaded.

A step-by-step guide to the art of getting rid of junk

Getting rid of mental chaos starts with taking small, well-thought-out moves. You don't have to clear out your whole mind at once. Instead, work on making room for understanding one thought at a time. How to do it:

The Brain Dump Method: Just Say It All

Get everything out of your head and write it down first. We refer to this as a "brain dump," which is an effective method for eliminating mental clutter.

Write down any ideas, worries, chores, or reminders that come to mind in a notebook or on a computer screen. Do not arrange or change it; just let it run.

Allowing your brain to think more freely is what makes this process work. It's easier for your brain to let go of your ideas when you write them down or draw them.

Let's say you're trying to sleep, but your brain keeps telling you to get food, email your boss, and make an appointment at the doctor. Don't keep turning over in your sleep; write it all down. You can calm down once it's on paper because you know it's safe.

Sort and set priorities

The next step after a brain dump is to put your thoughts in order. Sort the things on your list into groups, like "urgent tasks," "future goals," and "things to let go of."

Think about it:

- What should I pay attention to today?
- What can wait?
- What's not worth my time?

This helps you concentrate on what's important without having too much to handle at once.

Use tools for seeing.

People with ADHD do better with graphic tools. To keep track of your chores, you could use a planner, a schedule, or a digital app. It can be easier to see what's important at a glance if you use color-coding or sticky notes.

You could label important tasks with red, future tasks with yellow, and long-term goals with green. This clear vision helps clear up your mind and keep you focused on what's next.

Mindful check-ins should be done.

During the day, take a moment to talk to yourself. Question:

output:

output:

output:

output:

- What's making my mind so busy right now?
- Does this thought help me or hurt me?
- Mindful check-ins assist you in identifying and eliminating obstacles before they escalate.

How About an Emotional Mess?

Emotional baggage like shame, fear, or unresolved feelings that take up space in your thoughts are common types of mental clutter. This can feel especially heavy for women with ADHD because we tend to keep our problems to ourselves and blame ourselves for not living up to standards.

Start by being kind to yourself if you want to clear up your emotions. Remind yourself that it's okay to feel stressed out and that other people feel the same way. Writing in a journal or talking to a friend you trust can help you work through these feelings and let them go.

If you feel awful about not finishing a job, write down why it's difficult for you and what you can do to get back on track. Letting go of those feelings makes room for focus and action.

Questions People Ask About Getting Rid of Mental Clutter

"What if I can't stop thinking about it?""

This is fine. Your brain isn't a machine; it's always learning new things. Instead of trying to stop your thoughts from coming back, make it a habit to clean up your space every so often. Plan to dump your thoughts once a week or give yourself 10 minutes every night to think and get organized.

"What if I'm too stressed out to begin?""

Start out small. You don't have to get rid of everything in your mind at once. Focus on one thing at a time, like listing the things you need to do tomorrow or figuring out what's most important right now. Things need to get better, not better all the time.

How can clearing your mind transform your day?

When you clear your mind of clutter, you make room for peace, focus, and creativity. This will help you get things done, make choices, and enjoy the present time.

Imagine being able to focus on your work without having a hundred different thoughts pulling you in different ways. That's the power of clearing your mind: it makes your day clear and gives you control over your ADHD trip.

Now it's your turn to act.

Here's an easy way to start taking back your mind today:

- Step 1: Write down everything that comes to mind. Write down everything that's on your mind.
- Step 2: Divide your list into three groups: important, not important, and pressing.
- Step 3: Use a calendar or an app to make a clear list of your tasks.
- Step 4: Talk to yourself every day to clear your mind of new things.
- Step 5: Be pleased with your progress, no matter how little it is.

Mind clearing is a way to organize and take care of yourself. Setting aside time and room in your mind lets you concentrate on what really counts.

One thought at a time, let's get rid of the mess.

SIMPLE SYSTEMS THAT STICK ARE QUICK AND EASY WAYS TO GET ORGANIZED IN YOUR DAILY LIFE.

Does staying organized ever seem like a sandcastle that the tide washes away?

Regardless of the number of planners or applications you attempt, does it ever seem like maintaining organization is akin to constructing a sandcastle that the ocean sweeps away?

You're not by yourself. Sometimes it seems challenging for women with ADHD to stay organized. No matter how well you plan your day, things like forgotten meetings, misplaced keys, or the constant question, "What was I supposed to do next?" can cause you to lose focus. It can be frustrating and exhausting, making you doubt your life skills.

The truth is that regular ways of organizing don't work for people with ADHD. You don't need strict plans or planners that are color-coded. What you need are simple, adaptable systems that work for you, not the typical individual.

Why the old ways of dealing with ADHD don't work

Let's talk about why so many ways of organizing don't work for women with ADHD before we get to the answers. A well-known expert on ADHD, Dr. Edward Hallowell, says, "ADHD brains have trouble being consistent and following through, especially when systems are too complicated or dull."

Even if a standard planner looks appealing on paper, you probably won't use it if it doesn't challenge you or make you feel good. When you finally give up, you feel like you've failed, but the system really let you down.

You need methods that are straightforward to use, simple to keep up, and flexible enough to adapt to your changing hobbies and energy levels.

The power of visual organization is immense.

Making your planning visual is one of the best tricks for people with ADHD. It's true that "out of sight, out of mind," so keeping tasks and notes in a way that you can see and touch can make a big difference.

The Command Center was hacked.

Make a "command center" in your home—a place where you can see and take care of all the things you need every day. These things could be:
- A large calendar displays events and deadlines.
- Use a whiteboard to record daily tasks or notes.
- You can use hooks to hold bags, keys, or other items that you frequently misplace.
- A compact tray holds crucial documents such as bills and forms.
- This setup keeps everything in one place, so you can relax.

Imagine waking up and seeing a whiteboard with a clear outline of your day. Instead of rushing to figure out what's most important, you can focus immediately on the tasks at hand.

Chunking: Splitting up big tasks into smaller ones that you can handle

Have you ever struggled to start a large task, such as cleaning your house or preparing for an event? That's because people with ADHD have trouble breaking down big jobs into smaller steps that they can easily complete.

How to Hack: Chunking

"Chunking" refers to the process of breaking down large projects into smaller, more manageable pieces. Instead of writing "clean the house" on your to-do list, break it down into the following:
- Clear off the counters in the kitchen.
- Clean the floors.
- Sort the pillows in the living room.

You can handle each step, and crossing them off gives you a dopamine boost that keeps you going.

Things you can do:

Write down one big thing you've been putting off. Next, write down the first three steps you need to take to begin. Just pay attention to those steps. When you're done with them, move on to the next part.

The Two-Minute Rule: Stop Putting Things Off

Some jobs get piled up because we don't want to deal with them or find them interesting enough to prioritize. That's where the Two-Minute Rule comes in.

The Two-Minute Rule is the hack.

Do something right away if it takes less than two minutes, like answering an email, putting your shoes away, or starting the dishes. Leaving these little jobs undone often leads to extra mess, so doing them right away keeps your mind and space clear.

It's better to look through your mail right away when you walk in the door than to let it pile up on the counter. You won't have to deal with a bigger mess later because of the little work.

Batching: Make Doing the Same Things Faster

People with ADHD may feel tired when they have to do the same things over and over, like doing cleaning, cooking, or running errands. Batching is a great way to get things done quickly and easily.

"Task Batching" is the hack.

Putting together jobs that are similar will help you finish them faster. As an example:
- On Sunday, make all of your meals for the week.
- Don't spread out your tasks; do them all in one trip.
- Set up dates or calls that happen right after each other.

Batching cuts down on the number of times you have to switch gears, which is where people with ADHD often lose their focus and speed.

Things you can do:

This week, choose one type of jobs to do all at once, like making meals or running errands. Take note of how much easier your day goes when you put those things together.

Make places for everything

People with ADHD often have trouble remembering where they put their phone, keys, cash, or even important papers. How to solve it? Give everything its own "home."

What the Hack Does: Set Apart Areas

Give things that you use often a special place to go. Put them on hooks, bins, or trays to make them easy to get to and see. As an example:
- A hook for your keys by the door.
- A bin for charging and other tech on your desk.
- Something to put bills and important papers in.
- Putting things where they belong makes it easier to find what you need without spending time looking.

Making your to-do list fun

Truly, dull jobs are the worst for people with ADHD. What if we transformed those chores into a game?

The Hack: Making games

- Use tasks or rewards to make your list more fun and worthwhile. As an example:
- Check your time to see how fast you can do something.
- You'll get points for each thing you cross off, and when you hit a certain score, you'll deserve a prize.
- You can use apps like Habitica to make your work more like a game.
- Gamification uses your brain's love of new things and rewards to make even boring jobs feel fun.

Why being flexible is important

Because life and energy levels change all the time, rigid methods don't work well for ADHD brains. Flexibility—letting people make changes without feeling negative about it—is key to making a system last.

The Trick: The 80/20 Rule

Instead of trying to be great, focus on getting 80% of your work done. It's a positive sign if you get most things done. For the 20% that doesn't go as planned, be kind to yourself.

Things you can do:

Instead of dwelling on what you failed to complete, enjoy what you did at the end of the day. Things need to get better, not better all the time.

Your customized plan to succeed.

To get things done, stick to the plans that work best for you. Start small, try new things, and change them as needed. Here's a quick outline to get you started:

- Set up your command center: make a place where you can see all of your tasks and notes.
- Break up your big tasks into smaller steps that you can do.
- Batch jobs: To save time, group jobs that are similar together.
- Make your routine more like a game by adding fun and prizes to dull jobs.
- Don't be rigid; change your methods as your life does.

Your Way of Organizing

Remember that keeping prepared isn't about following someone else's plan; it's about making your own. You're not just living when you accept that you have ADHD and build methods around its strengths.

Your life should be clear, easy to handle, and in line with who you are. In small steps, one system at a time.

Emotional Resilience Made Easy: How to Get Over Rejection and Overwhelm

"Does every word from someone you care about ever be like a bomb going off in your head?"

You know the weight of rejection sensitivity and overload if you've ever gone crazy over a casual comment or played over a mistake in your head until it became unbearable. For women with ADHD, these emotional problems aren't just annoying once in a while; they can feel like storms that never end. But here's the truth: your feelings may feel like a wave, but they are what makes you strong. You can learn to handle those waves, become stronger, and feel mentally well if you have the right tools.

Why it's so hard to deal with rejection

A common but often ignored part of ADHD is rejection sensitivity distress (RSD). Dr. William Dodson, an expert on ADHD, says that RSD is "an intense emotional response to perceived or actual rejection, criticism, or failure." Even small slights, like a friend not replying to a text, can make someone feel bad about themselves for a long time after they should not.

This stronger emotional reaction is connected to how people with ADHD handle dopamine, which is a chemical that controls mood and makes us feel good. Lack of dopamine can make feelings more direct and uncensored.

There's no need to believe it or worry that you might be "too sensitive." Your brain is wired to feel deeply, which can be overwhelming but also gives you a huge capacity for sensitivity, love, and connection.

Why is it so easy to feel overwhelmed?

When you have rejection sensitivity and the normal problems that come with ADHD, like brain failure and time-blindness, it's no surprise that you feel overwhelmed all the time. It can be challenging to keep up with work, relationships, and personal goals at the same time. This can leave you stuck in decision-making or full of self-doubt.

"Why can't I handle this like everyone else?" you might ask yourself. However, she pointed out that you are unique in your own way. Your brain handles information, feelings, and tasks in a unique way. This isn't a weakness; it's just a difference that needs a different approach.

How to Build Emotional Strength Step-By-Step

To overcome rejection sensitivity and overwhelm, you don't need to suppress your emotions. Instead, you need to learn how to work with them. Here is a plan that will help you become more emotionally strong:

Figure out what sets you off.

Being aware is the first step in dealing with emotional overwhelm. Pay attention to what makes you feel very rejected or stressed. It could be a mean comment from a coworker, a fight with a close friend or family member, or even the way you talk to yourself.

In a journal or paper, write down the things that set you off. Doing this regularly helps you see trends and get a better sense of what needs your attention.

Let's say it hurts you when your partner doesn't answer your text right away. Realizing that this is a trigger lets you deal with it quietly instead of getting angry or upset at the time.

Take a moment to name how you feel.

It's easy to lose yourself in the intensity of rejection or overwhelm. Instead, pause and name what you're feeling. Are you sad? Frustrated? Anxious? Just naming your emotions can help you separate them from your actions.

Neuroscience backs this method, known as "naming to tame." By labeling your feelings, you engage the rational part of your brain, lowering the strength of the emotional reaction.

Reframe Your Inner Narrative

Often, rejection sensitivity is accompanied by a harsh internal critic. You might think, "I'm not talented enough" or "Everyone must be upset at me." But these thoughts are often errors, not facts.

Practice changing these beliefs. Instead of, "I failed, so I'm a failure," try, "I made a mistake, but that doesn't define me." This shift helps you see situations more clearly and react with self-compassion.

Things you can do:

The next time you find yourself in a negative cycle, challenge the thought.

Is this thought based on truth or fear?

In this case, how would I talk to a friend?

Be kind when you set limits.

Taking on too much or trying to meet everyone's needs can make you feel overwhelmed. Being able to say "no" or delegate chores is healthy, not selfish.

Start out small. Pick an area where you feel overworked and set a limit. You might decide not to answer work emails after 7 p.m., for instance. You could also inform a friend that you need some time to rest.

Use techniques that calm you down right now.

Having a variety of ways to calm down can be very helpful when feelings are too much to handle. Here are some methods to try:

Inhale for four counts, hold for four counts, and then release for four counts. This makes your heart beat more slowly and calms you down.

Focus on your senses by listing five things you can see, four things you can touch, three things you can hear, two things you can smell, and one thing you can taste.

Moving your body: A short walk or even just wringing your hands out can help you get rid of stress and clear your mind.

Questions People Often Ask About Being Emotionally Strong

"What will happen if I can't hold back?"

It's okay for this to happen. Being emotionally strong doesn't mean being perfect; it means learning and getting better over time. If you act quickly, think about what you did and how you could handle it better next time.

"How do I tell other people about RSD?"

Sometimes it helps to talk about what's going on with people you trust. You could say, "Because of how my brain works, I feel rejection very strongly." Please understand that I don't always make sense, and thank you for your patience.

How can being strong transform your day?

You could wake up every day knowing that you are ready to handle anything that comes your way. You don't spiral after a tough talk; instead, you take a moment to name your thoughts and change the way you're telling the story. When you have too many things to do, you set limits and move forward in small, doable steps.

Being emotionally strong doesn't mean you'll never be hurt or stressed again. It means you'll deal with those feelings with grace and strength, seeing problems as chances to grow.

Your Plan for Emotional Strength

To start gaining emotional strength today, here's an easy plan:
- Find Your Triggers: Write down the things that make you feel rejected or overwhelmed.
- Practice Naming Your Feelings: When certain events happen, take a moment to name how you're feeling.
- Challenge Negative Thoughts: Instead of being tough with yourself, say nice, realistic things.
- Set Small Boundaries: Pick one area where you can say "no" or give work to someone else.
- Create a set of tools for relaxation by trying out different ways to breathe, settle yourself, and move.

You're stronger than you think.

Being sensitive to rejection and feeling overwhelmed don't make you who you are; they're just problems you can learn to solve. Emotional strength becomes second nature with practice and patience. This gives you the confidence to handle life's ups and downs.

You are not your feelings; you have control over them. Let's take it one step at a time.

How to Handle Hormonal Changes: The Hormone- ADHD Link

"Do you ever feel like your ADHD is really bad around certain times of the month, making it impossible to do even simple things?""

If your mood, energy, or ability to focus changes a lot for no reason, it may not be just your ADHD talking. It could be your hormones. For women with ADHD, changes in hormones can make symptoms worse and make an already difficult situation even more difficult to deal with.

Figuring out how your hormones affect your ADHD is not only helpful, it changes everything. You can plan for, adapt to, and handle these changes better if you know how they affect your brain and body.

How hormones affect ADHD signs and symptoms

There is a strong scientific link between hormones and ADHD. The hormone estrogen controls many of your body's functions. It also plays a major role in the production of dopamine, a neurotransmitter that ADHD brains already have trouble controlling.

Dr. Patricia Quinn, an expert on ADHD in women, says, "Estrogen raises the activity of dopamine and serotonin, which are important for mood, motivation, and attention." ADHD signs often get worse when estrogen levels change.

Think about how you feel when you have your period. During the first half, called the follicular phase, estrogen levels rise, which can make it easier to concentrate and have more energy. But when estrogen levels drop in the second half (the luteal phase), you may feel more sensitive to emotions, have brain fog, and have trouble focusing.

How to Get Around the Monthly Shockwave

But how can you deal with these natural changes in hormones without feeling like they're taking over your life? The important thing is to know your cycle and make plans based on that.

Step 1: Keep track of your symptoms and cycle.

Start by keeping track of both your ADHD symptoms and your period. When you feel different ways on different days, write them down in a book or an app.

For instance, you may find that the week before your period is the worst for putting things off or the most sensitive to emotions. Knowing these patterns allows you to prepare in advance.

Step 2: Schedule Around Your Strengths

Once you discover your hormonal highs and lows, plan your jobs accordingly. Schedule hard work, artistic projects, or social commitments during high-energy phases, and keep low-energy phases for rest or routine jobs.

Example: If you know your focus is sharpest during the follicular phase, use that time to handle complex jobs. Save jobs like organizing or picking up on emails for the luteal phase, when brain fog might make deep focus harder.

The Impact of Life Stages on Hormonal Shifts

Hormonal changes don't stop with your monthly cycle—they grow throughout your life, changing your ADHD in different ways.

During and after giving birth

Having more estrogen during pregnancy can sometimes help ADHD symptoms, making a person feel surprisingly calm and focused. But estrogen levels drop a lot after giving birth, which can make ADHD symptoms worse and raise the risk of postpartum sadness.

If you're managing parenting, give yourself grace. Recognize that these changes are brief and seek support from loved ones, therapists, or ADHD experts when needed.

Perimenopause and Menopause

Hormones change in unpredictable ways during perimenopause, the years before menopause. As estrogen levels drop, ADHD signs like confusion, irritability, and emotional sensitivity often get worse.

A psychologist who specializes in ADHD in women, Dr. Ellen Littman, says, "Many women are diagnosed with ADHD for the first time during perimenopause because the drop in estrogen makes symptoms they've been hiding for years worse."

Know that you're not the only one going through this time. Hormone replacement therapy (HRT), changes to your lifestyle, and techniques designed just for people with

ADHD can help you get through this shift more easily.

How to Keep Your Balance

Taking care of the link between hormones and ADHD needs more than one method. Here are some useful ways to keep your body and mind in sync:

Feed your body with food.

Keeping your mood and energy levels stable depends a lot on what you eat. Foods that are high in omega-3 fatty acids (salmon, flaxseeds), magnesium (spinach, nuts), and vitamin B6 (bananas, chicken) can help keep your hormones in balance.

If you're having PMS and want something sweet, choose a piece of dark chocolate or a bunch of nuts. These foods will fill your cravings and give your body nutrients at the same time.

Make a moving plan.

Dopamine and serotonin levels rise when you exercise, which makes you feel better and helps you concentrate. When you have a lot of energy, try doing more intense workouts like running or dancing. When you feel tired, doing gentle yoga or stretching can help you get your energy back.

Put rest and recovery first.

You have to get enough sleep, especially when your hormones are changing. Set up a routine before bed that helps you sleep well, like limiting screen time, using quiet essential oils, or listening to relaxing music.

Things you can do:

If you have trouble sleeping when your hormones drop, try a weighted blanket or slow breathing to calm your body and mind.

Count on supplements and help

If the changes in your hormones are too much for you to handle, talk to your doctor about taking magnesium or omega-3 supplements or even hormonal treatments. Medications made just for ADHD or techniques that help you be more aware can also help balance the effects of hormonal changes.

Questions People Often Ask About ADHD and Hormones

"Why do my ADHD symptoms get worse some months but not others?"“

Hormonal changes happen naturally, and the strength of them can change from cycle to cycle. These benefits can be boosted by things like worry, diet, and sleep.

"Can birth control help with ADHD symptoms caused by hormones?"“

Hormonal birth control can help some women keep their estrogen levels steady, which can lower symptom changes. It is not, however, a one-size-fits-all answer. Talk to your doctor about what will work best for your body.

How Knowing About Hormones Can Change Your Day

Imagine being able to figure out why you feel energized or foggy when you wake up and having a plan for how to deal with it. Figuring out the link between hormones and ADHD won't get rid of problems; it will help you plan for and deal with them.

You'll feel more in control, less stressed, and better able to handle life's demands when you match your routine with your body's natural processes.

Plan for Hormones and ADHD

Here is a quick guide on how to start dealing with hormonal changes correctly:

Track Your Cycle: Write down your symptoms and energy levels every day or use an app to do this.

Plan accordingly: Put hard jobs on your list for times when you have a lot of energy and give yourself time to rest when you don't.

Pay attention to your nutrition: eat foods that balance your hormones.

Move Your Body: Make sure your workouts are a good fit for your energy level.

Get help: Talk to your doctor about treatments, vitamins, or medicines that might help.

Accept your natural rhythms.

It's not that your hormones are against you; they're just how your body works. If you know how they affect your ADHD, you can make your life feel more calm, purposeful, and powerful.

Together, we will navigate these changes and establish a practice that benefits both your brain and body. You can do this.

MAKING SMALL CHANGES THAT ADD UP TO BIG WINS INVOLVES FORMING HABITS THAT ARE BENEFICIAL FOR PEOPLE WITH ADHD.

"Do you ever feel like you try to form habits but fail before they even start to grow?"

You're not by yourself. Developing new habits can be challenging for women with ADHD. You start a new habit one day and are sure that this time it will work. But it ends after a week or even just a few days, leaving you upset and wondering if you'll ever be able to follow through.

The truth is, people with ADHD don't benefit from regular advice on habit building. No, you don't need more control or willpower. What you need are techniques that work with your ADHD and your mind. Learn how to make small changes that add up to big wins by starting small and sticking with it.

Why people with ADHD can't keep up old habits

Developing habits requires stability, routine, and waiting to get what you want, which are all things that ADHD brains naturally struggle with. A well-known ADHD expert, Dr. Russell Barkley, says, "ADHD hurts executive function, which makes it harder to keep up with things like planning, sequencing, and self-monitoring."

For instance, neurotypical advice might tell you to make a morning practice that includes working out, meditating, and writing in a diary before you start your day. But for someone with ADHD, even the easiest plan can become a huge hassle because they have to remember the steps, stay focused, and stay away from things that might get in the way.

If you've ever felt bad about not keeping a habit, it's not because you're lazy or lack control. The system wasn't made to work with your brain.

Start small and give rewards often to help kids with ADHD form positive habits.

To make habits that last, you need to break them down into small steps and give yourself benefits right away. Because people with ADHD need new things, dopamine, and positive feedback, the goal is to make habits feel doable and satisfying from the start.

Step 1: Pick one small change.

It's easy to get burned out when you try to change everything about your life at once. Instead, pick one small habit that you want to work on.

Instead of promising to work out for 30 minutes every day, try stretching for five minutes or going for a short walk around the block. If a habit is small, it's easier to do and more likely to stick with you.

Step 2: Connect your habit to something you know.

It's easier to form a new habit when you connect it to something you already do. This is known as "habit stacking," and James Clear made it famous in his book Atomic Habits.

Put a glass of water next to your coffee maker and sip from it while you wait for your coffee to brew. This will help you drink more water. Making coffee, which is already a habit, sets off the new habit of drinking water.

Dopamine Boosts Can Help You Gain Speed

People with ADHD are built to look for benefits right away, so giving your habits a small dopamine boost can help them stick. It's not necessary to go all out; it only needs to feel good or fun.

Things you can do:

While you clean, put on your favorite music.

Keep track of your progress with a sticker chart or an app (yes, even adults like sticker charts!).

Enjoy a treat, like a chocolate bar or a five-minute break, when you reach a small goal.

These benefits help you keep up the habit and keep your mind active.

How to Get Past Common ADHD Habit-Building Problems

"What if I forget to do the habit?""

People with ADHD often forget things, but visual aids can help. Put sticky notes where they will be seen, set your phone's alarm, or use an app with alerts to help you remember.

For instance, if you want to take your daily medicine, put the bottle next to your toothbrush. Seeing it helps you remember to do it and connects the habit to a pattern you already have.

"What if I stop wanting to do it?"“

Motivation comes and goes, especially for ADHD people. Focus on making the habit as easy and fun as possible instead of depending on your willpower. Don't be hard on yourself if you miss a day. Just start over the next day.

If working out seems too hard, try having a dance party in your living room or doing a quick stretch while you watch TV.

How Making Little Changes Can Help You Win Big

Focusing on small changes that you make over time will help you form new habits. Things that don't seem important right now could make your life much better weeks, months, or years from now.

Let us say you start by making it a habit to drink one more glass of water every day. You'll feel more hydrated over time, which will give you more energy and help you concentrate. That energy gives you more understanding about your work, which makes you feel better about your abilities. Every part of your life can be affected by a small change.

Tools for building habits that are good for people with ADHD

To make it easy to form habits, here are some tools and tips:

Making your habits fun

Keep track of your runs or play a game with a friend based on your habits. When you finish jobs in apps like Habitica, you get points, which makes the process fun and satisfying.

Set timers

People with ADHD often have trouble keeping track of time, so a timer can help you stay on track. Set a 10-minute timer to start a new job or clean up your space, for example.

Trackers that show progress

Make a chart to keep track of your habits. To keep going, you need to see your progress. Crossing off a job gives you an adrenaline boost.

A Day in the Life of Habits That Are Good for People with ADHD

Imagine starting your day with a habit that is easy and makes you feel good. While you wait for your coffee, you might take a sip of water and then stretch for two minutes to wake up your body. You set timers to help you stay on track and enjoy every small victory because you know that each step is important.

Because you're building a routine that works for you, you feel like you got a lot done by the end of the day. Not because you did everything perfectly.

Your Plan for Making Habits Stick

Are you interested in forming habits that will assist individuals with ADHD? A simple framework is shown below:

Choose One Small Habit: Pay attention to one small change you want to make.

Hook it up to a routine: Connect the new habit to something you already do.

Prize Yourself: Give yourself a small prize right away to help you keep up the habit.

You can keep track of your progress with a chart, an app, or a paper.

Don't be rigid: missed a day? Not a problem. Start over tomorrow.

Little steps lead to big wins.

When you have ADHD, building habits isn't about being perfect; it's about making progress. You can make a habit that feels sustainable and powerful if you focus on small, doable changes and enjoy each step forward.

You're not just making habits; you're making a life that works for you. Let's begin slowly, keep going, and enjoy each victory along the way.

Chapter 2: Thriving in Your Daily Routine

Here are the crucial takeaways from Chapter 2:

• Decluttering Your Mind: Clear mental chaos with tools like brain dumps, mindful check-ins, and prioritizing tasks into manageable steps.

• Simple Systems That Stick: Use ADHD-friendly strategies like visual reminders, task batching, and habit stacking to create organization that lasts.

• Emotional Resilience Made Easy: Manage rejection sensitivity and stress by naming your feelings, changing negative thoughts, and building a calming toolbox.

• The Hormone-ADHD Connection: Understand how hormonal changes impact your ADHD and plan your habits around energy highs and lows.

• Building ADHD-Friendly Habits: Start small, anchor habits to existing routines, and enjoy each small win to build lasting, empowering changes.

Now that you've laid the base for thriving in your daily routine, it's time to focus on your relationships. Chapter 3 will explore how to build important relationships, handle social dynamics, and improve bonds with the people who matter most. Let's jump right in!

CHAPTER 3: BUILDING MEANINGFUL CONNECTIONS

"True connection starts with understanding yourself—and sharing that understanding with others."

IMPROVING YOUR RELATIONSHIPS: HOW TO CLEARLY STATE YOUR NEEDS

"The biggest communication mistake is assuming others already know what we need."

I used to believe that someone should understand my needs if they truly cared about me. When they didn't, I would feel angry or even hurt, believing they weren't paying attention or didn't value me enough. It wasn't until a friend softly said, "I can't read your mind," that I realized the problem. "Tell me how I can help." I realized the problem wasn't their lack of care but my lack of communication.

Women with ADHD may struggle to connect with their loved ones when they don't understand them, are emotionally sensitive, or feel inadequate. However, being clear and kind about your needs can strengthen your relationships.

Why does it seem more difficult to discuss needs when you have ADHD?

You're not the only one who has had trouble saying what they need. Because ADHD affects your brain function, it can be challenging to even figure out what you need, let alone say it. You may overshare or act fine to avoid disagreements.

A well-known expert on ADHD, Dr. Edward Hallowell, says, "People with ADHD often think they don't have the right to ask for what they need, which makes them angry and frustrated." Does this sound like you?

Learning to speak well starts with an awareness of your needs. Anyone else should be able to hear and understand you.

Know what you want before you talk to someone.

Clarity requires knowing what you want to say before saying it. This can be especially challenging for people with ADHD because their minds are often full of different feelings and thoughts.

Things you can do:

Pause and Think: When you're mad or angry, stop and ask yourself, "What am I really feeling right now?" What do I need to feel cared for?"

Write It Down: Writing down your thoughts can help you sort them out and figure out what's most important. For instance, if you have too many jobs around the house, you could say, "I need help with laundry and dishes this week."

Being clear doesn't mean being perfect; it means getting to what will motivate and balance you.

Say what you want to say with "I" statements.

Once you know what you need, you should tell someone about it in a clear and polite way. You can say what you want to say without looking accusatory or defensive by using "I" words.

Such as:

Instead of saying, "You never listen to me," consider saying, "I feel unheard when you interrupt me." Could we focus on allowing each other to finish?

This method changes the attention from blaming to working together, which makes it more likely that the other person will want to cooperate.

Be clear and doable.

Being too unclear is one of the most common ways to mess up conversation. When you say, "I need help," the other person may be clueless. Be clear about what you need and how they can help you instead.

Such as:

If you feel like you have too many things to do as a parent, don't say, "I can't do this anymore." Instead, say, "I need you to take over bath time and bedtime on Tuesday and Thursday so I can have some time to myself."

To get someone to help you in a useful way, make sure your requests are clear and specific.

Start a conversation with both sides.

Just as important as saying what you need is listening to the other person. Relationships work best when both people understand each other, and making time for conversation helps people connect.

Things you can do:

Tell Them What You Need: Once you've communicated your needs, solicit their feedback. "How does that sound to you?" Or, "What do you think about this idea?"

Active listening means that when they speak, you should pay attention to what they are saying without talking back or thinking about what you will say next. Saying things like, "It sounds like you're worried about timing," back to them shows that you heard them and care about their point of view.

What Should I Do If They Don't Respond Well?

Even if you mean well, not everyone will respond as you want. They might be angry, defensive, or not sure how to help. This doesn't mean you failed to communicate; it just means you need to give the talk more thought and time.

Things you can do:

Keep your cool. If you're feeling angry or upset, take a break and talk about it again later. "I think we're both feeling overwhelmed," they said. Could we take a break and revisit this later?

Reframe and Try Again: If they didn't get what you were trying to say, say it again in a different way. Like, "I don't mean to criticize." "I just need help because I'm feeling really stretched thin."

Over time, patience and effort can help people understand each other better.

How effective communication makes relationships stronger

Building trust and mutual respect starts with being clear about what you need. Supporters won't have to guess how to help you because you've already told them.

Imagine that you and your partner both feel seen, heard, and valued in your partnership. When things are hard, you don't have to be afraid to ask for help. They know you're there for them when they're having a tough time. This isn't just wishful thinking; it's the result of clear, conscious conversation.

Your Action Plan for Communication

Here is a step-by-step plan that you can use right away to make your relationships stronger:

Think About Your Needs: Write down how you feel and what you need for five minutes.

Use "I" statements: Spend some time putting your wants into words that focus on how you feel and how to solve the problem, rather than who is to blame.

Be Clear: Divide your desires into manageable requests.

Encourage conversation: Ask what the other person thinks and listen.

Keep an open mind. If things don't go as planned, change the subject and try again later.

Your opinion is important.

If you want better relationships, you must value your opinions and needs. You are empowered to form bonds through trust, understanding, and mutual assistance.

Don't forget that positive conversation isn't about being perfect; it's about making progress. Every talk is a chance to get to know the important people in your life better. You can do this.

Finding Your ADHD Tribe: Making Friends and Communities That Support You

"There was a time when I thought I had to deal with my ADHD in silence." I had no idea how much finding people who really understood me would change my life.

As a child, I frequently experienced feelings of isolation. Things that other people thought were simple were challenging for me, and I had to work twice as hard just to keep up. Advice from other people, even when they meant well, often didn't help. It wasn't until I encountered other individuals with ADHD that I realized I wasn't flawed; I was simply unique.

Having an ADHD family, or a group of people who really get what you're going through, can change your life. These links help you and give you a sense of belonging and power, which is healthy. Let's talk about how to find people who understand ADHD and help you make friends and grow your community.

Why is community important for women with ADHD?

ADHD can make people feel alone, especially women. Society often expects us to balance many responsibilities, like work, relationships, and family, while keeping calm and organized. When ADHD makes these tasks seem impossible, it's easy to feel like you're failing.

"Connection is one of the most powerful tools for managing ADHD," says Dr. Ned Hallowell, a well-known ADHD expert. Isolation makes problems worse, but society helps people learn and grow.

When you're with people who understand your problems and praise your skills, you get more than just friends. You get power, confidence, and a new point of view.

Step 1: Know how valuable your tribe is.

To begin the process of creating an ADHD group, you must understand the importance of doing so. Communities and friendships that support each other offer:

When someone says "me too" to your problems, it helps you remember that you're not the only one.

Helpful Hints: Individuals with ADHD often generate innovative ideas due to their personal experiences.

When things get tough, your group can support and remind you of your strengths.

Not only are these relationships nice, they're also important for your mental and emotional health.

Step 2: Look for people with similar ideas.

It doesn't have to be difficult to find people who have ADHD. These methods can help you find others in similar situations:

1. Community sites online

There are a lot of support groups, platforms, and social media pages for people with ADHD on the internet. There are busy ADHD groups on Facebook, Reddit, and even Instagram, where people can share their stories, ask questions, and learn from each other.

If you join a Facebook group like "Women with ADHD," you can get daily support, ideas, and motivation. You'll realize many women have gone through what you have.

2. Attend events and meetups in your area.

If you'd rather talk to someone in person, look for ADHD support groups or classes in your area. Meetups are events in many places where you can get to know other people in a friendly, open setting.

3. Communities Based on Interests

You don't have to limit your ADHD group to just people with ADHD. You can also meet intriguing people by joining a group based on your hobbies, like a book club, art class, or exercise group.

Things you can do:

Take a small step first, like joining an online group or going to an event in your area. Don't forget that making relationships takes time, so be kind to yourself.

Step 3: Take care of your new friends.

Creating relationships is one thing, but taking care of them is quite another. Having ADHD can make it challenging to keep friends, especially if you have trouble remembering things or managing your time. You can, however, make your interactions stronger with a little effort.

Things you can do:

Tell the truth: Tell your new friends that you have ADHD. This helps people have fair goals and understand each other better.

Set Reminders: To set up regular coffee dates or check-ins, use your phone or notebook. This will help you stay in touch even when things get busy.

Honor Small Acts: A quick text, a clever joke, or a note with lots of thought can show that you care.

For instance, if you meet someone at a local ADHD group and express, "I really enjoyed our conversation," send them a message. "Let's get coffee soon."

Step 4: Create a network that will help you.

Your group of people with ADHD doesn't have to just be friends. You can build a strong base by getting help from a variety of people, such as mentors, coaches, and experts.

Helpers and examples

Find people who can motivate and assist with ADHD. This could be a priest, a teacher, or even an online friend you look up to.

Friends and family.

Some family members may not understand ADHD, but finding those who will listen and help can strengthen your network.

An encouraging sister may not have ADHD themselves, but they can help you stay on track with your goals and give you support.

Questions People Ask About Finding Their Tribe

"What if I'm afraid to put myself out there?"

Meeting new people can cause anxiety, particularly if you've experienced judgment or misinterpretation in the past. Start small by leaving a comment on a post in an online group or going to a social get-together. Remind yourself that the people you're meeting are probably going through the same things and want help too.

"What if I don't get along with anybody right away?"

It takes time to make relationships that matter. Don't give up if a certain person or group doesn't seem like the right fit. Keep looking around until you find a neighborhood that makes you feel like you belong.

Discovering your tribe can transform your life.

Consider surrounding yourself with friends who share in your successes, empathize with your struggles, and provide helpful tips tailored to your ADHD brain. They help you remember that you're not alone when you're feeling stressed. They cheer the most when you're doing well.

Finding your group makes your interactions better, but it also makes your life better in general. You'll feel less alone, more encouraged, and more free to enjoy your own unique journey.

How do you plan to find and build your ADHD tribe?

To start building your group, here are some steps you can take:

Join an online group. Look for groups for people with ADHD on Facebook, Reddit, or Instagram and say hello.

Go to an Event Near You: Look around your area for support groups, classes, or meetups.

Reach out to a new person. Send a message or call someone you like and set up a time to talk again.

Stay Connected: Remind yourself to keep up with relationships by doing small, kind things.

Add teachers, coaches, and friends who can help and guide you to your network.

You're Not By Yourself

Finding your ADHD family is about building a network of people who can help you succeed, not just friends. You're never on this journey by yourself if you have an online community, a neighborhood group, or a single friend who "gets it."

Your group will support you, listen to your concerns, and keep you going. Let's get to work on it together.

ADHD in Love: How to Get Through Romantic Relationships with Understanding

"Before my ADHD caused misunderstandings that love alone couldn't fix, I thought love was enough to get through any problem in a relationship."

In a previous relationship, I recall my partner becoming upset with me because I neglected to order our anniversary dinner. Since I'd been anticipating it all week, I cared. My ADHD brain became overwhelmed by all the work tasks and mental clutter. We were fighting that night, and I felt like I had failed as a partner. At the time, I was unaware that having well-defined goals alone is not sufficient to navigate a love relationship with ADHD. You also need to understand, communicate, and work together.

You're not the only one who has felt that way. Despite their challenges, ADHDers can benefit from relationships. You can build a relationship that lasts and gives you a lot of joy if you have the right tools and attitudes.

Why ADHD can hurt romantic relationships

ADHD changes the way you think, feel, and act, and those changes will easily show up in your interactions. Impulsivity, forgetfulness, and being too sensitive to other people's feelings can make things worse between you, but focus, imagination, and understanding can make things better.

One of the top experts on ADHD in relationships, Dr. Melissa Orlov, says, "The ADHD partner often unintentionally creates patterns that feel unfair to the non-ADHD partner, leading to misunderstandings and resentment." For example, your partner may feel neglected when you forget important dates or have trouble keeping your promises, even though that wasn't your intention.

The first step to breaking these habits is understanding them. Let's talk about how you can deal with these problems with kindness and respect.

Step 1: Talk about ADHD openly with others.

One of the hardest things about relationships with ADHD is that people don't always understand. Your partner may perceive your ADHD-like behaviors as signs of boredom or laziness, despite your unique wiring.

Things you can do:

Talk to someone about your ADHD in an open and honest way. Tell your partner how helping you makes you feel. You could say something like, "I forget things sometimes, even when they're important to me." I do care; I simply require reminders to remain focused.

It's not about making excuses in this talk; it's about building knowledge and empathy.

Step 2: Deal with your feelings together

People who have rejection sensitivity dysphoria (RSD) can feel terrible about even small disagreements. Some potential outcomes include overreacting to minor criticisms or experiencing guilt following an argument.

Let's say your partner casually mentions that you haven't finished the dishes. When you hear a simple comment, your ADHD brain might think, "I'm failing as a partner." This can make you protective or withdrawn, which creates a gap.

Things you can do:

Before You React: When you're feeling angry or upset, take a deep breath and ask yourself, "What did they say? How do I feel?"“

Say What You Feel: Tell your partner how their words make you feel without blaming them. For instance, "I know you didn't mean it this way, but when you brought up the dishes, I felt judged."

Find Comfort: When you need comfort, ask for it. "I love you, and we'll figure this out" is a wonderful way to help someone with RSD feel better.

Step 3: Fill in the blanks with tools

People with ADHD often forget things and have trouble telling time, which can make relationships tense. Your partner might feel compelled to constantly inform you about things or shoulder a greater emotional burden.

Things you can do:

Use shared calendars. Google Calendar and other similar tools can help you keep track of your plans and cut down on the need for prompts. Set reminders for important events like anniversary nights or date nights.

Handle Tasks Smartly: If some of your tasks are too much for you, split them up in a way that plays to your skills with your partner. You could focus on artistic tasks while your partner handles tasks that require more care.

Set up visual reminders: Sticky notes, whiteboards, or phone alerts can help you remember things without having to rely on your partner alone.

Tools like these are meant to help you create processes that work for both of you, not avoid duty.

Step 4: Celebrate the positive aspects of ADHD with love

ADHD can create challenges, but it can also strengthen love relationships in remarkable ways. Your enthusiasm, imagination, and love can make your relationship exciting and joyful.

Because you can focus very hard, you can turn a simple date night into an exciting adventure full of careful details that your partner will never forget. Because you have empathy, you can really feel what they're feeling, which makes them feel seen and respected.

Use these skills and tell your partner how much you value them. There are many unique and memorable ways to show your love, such as with a handwritten note, an act of kindness, or a surprise date.

Step 5: If you need help, get professional help.

ADHD can make relationships difficult, especially if there have been long-term fights or anger. A therapist or counselor who specializes in ADHD can help you deal with these situations by giving you useful tools and information.

Things you can do:

Look for couples therapy classes that address issues that arise with ADHD.

With a partner, read books or go to classes about ADHD.

During treatment, collaborate as a team and concentrate on improving rather than assigning blame.

"With the right help, couples can move from being angry at each other to working together, making a relationship that works for both of them," says Dr. Orlov.

Questions People Often Ask About ADHD in Love

"What if my partner does not suffer from ADHD?"

Getting educated is very important. Share things like stories or movies that talk about how ADHD affects relationships. Clear up any confusion, encourage questions, and talk about feelings.

"How do I deal with feeling guilty about having ADHD?"

It's normal to feel guilty, but it's not helpful. Instead of dwelling on your mistakes, focus on improving. Don't forget that every relationship has problems. Yours are just different.

How knowing each other changes relationships

When you're honest, understanding, and open to change in your relationship, you make room for a stronger bond. ADHD doesn't have to be a problem between you and your partner. You can see it as a chance to learn, grow, and make your relationship special.

Imagine being in a relationship where you both feel supported and understood. Together, they navigate through challenges without blaming others. Love blossoms when you embrace ADHD's lessons together, not because of it.

How do you plan to handle love when you have ADHD?

Here are some steps you can take to make your relationship stronger:

Ask your partner to talk about ADHD and how it affects them.

Make Tools Together: To ease stress, use calendars, notes, and shared tasks.

Practice being emotionally aware by pausing, thinking, and talking about your thoughts in a healthy way.

Lean Into Your Strengths: Enjoy the unique ways that ADHD makes your relationship better.

Get Help When You Need It: Don't be afraid to get help from a professional if you need advice or ideas.

Love that makes sense

ADHD makes it difficult to date, but it's possible. You can build a strong and satisfying relationship with your partner if you are patient, talk to each other, and are willing to grow together.

Love is about getting along, understanding, and being there every day without being perfect. And you have everything you need to make your love grow.

PARENTING WITH ADHD: HOW TO DO WELL AS A PARENT IF YOU HAVE ADHD

"One day I realized I wasn't just taking care of my own ADHD; I was also raising little people who needed me to guide them, love them, and keep it together." It seemed like an impossible act of balance.

Everyone finds parenting challenging, but if you have ADHD, it can feel like you're balancing a hundred lit torches. It's possible to feel split between the chaos in your mind and the confusion of living in a house. You might feel awful all the time if you forget about a school event or lose your cool over a small thing. The truth is that having ADHD does not make you a negative parent. In fact, it gives you special skills that can make you stand out.

As a mom of a child with ADHD, let's talk about how to find balance, let go of guilt, and make the family relationship work for everyone.

The Battle of the ADHD Parent

One of the hardest things about being a parent of a child with ADHD is that your mind is always full. Keeping track of all the tasks, such as remembering meetings, meals, and projects, can be challenging. It's straightforward to think that you're not living up to the "ideal parent" when your ADHD gets in the way.

A well-known expert on ADHD, Dr. Edward Hallowell, says, "Parents with ADHD often have to deal with their own symptoms while also trying to meet their children's needs." But with the right steps, they can create a welcoming, supportive environment for everyone.

Have you ever thought, "How can I be the parent my kids need when I'm having a hard time myself?"Know this: you're doing more than you think, and by making a few changes, you can really do well.

Step 1: Stop trying to be perfect.

Losing the unrealistic expectation of perfection is the first step to success as an ADHD parent. Nobody is perfect as a parent, ADHD or not. Trying to be perfect will only make you exhausted and harsh on yourself.

Things you can do:

Focus on Connection Over Perfection: Your kids don't need a perfect parent; they need one who loves them. It's more important to have regular, small times of connection, like reading a bedtime story or laughing together, than to have a perfectly planned routine.

Enjoy the little things: Did you remember to pack their lunch today? Give yourself a high five. Did you apologize for your anger? That's progress. Instead of dwelling on what you failed to do, focus on what you did.

2: Make routines that work for people with ADHD.

Traditional parenting tips often emphasize routines, but kids with ADHD do best when they can be flexible. It's important to create frameworks that are simple, flexible, and straightforward to keep up with.

Things you can do:

Utilize visual schedules: Create a family calendar or plan that outlines daily tasks, enabling you and your children to stay organized without relying solely on memory.

Divide tasks into smaller pieces: Divide large parenting responsibilities into manageable steps. Instead of telling them, "Clean your room," take it one step at a time: "Let's start by picking up the toys."

Anchor New Habits to Things You Already Do: Connect your new habits to things you already do. One idea is to go over the day's plans with your kids while you're making coffee in the morning.

These habits don't need to be strict; they just need to be enough to keep everyone on track.

Step 3: Adopt the positive things about your ADHD.

ADHD presents challenges, yet it also enhances your potential as a fun and engaging parent due to your creative, energetic, and innovative thinking.

Such as:

Because you act on impulse, you might end up on adventures you didn't plan, like a dance party in the living room or a trip to the park. Your kids will remember these times for a long time.

Things you can do:

Lean Into Your Creativity: To make boring things more fun, use your imagination. Turn chores or homework into an interactive game or story.

Be Present: If you have ADHD, it can be challenging to concentrate, but your attention is at its best when you're fully involved. In your alone time, use this to connect with your kids.

Step 4: Set up a System of Support

You don't need to do this by yourself. Building a network of support can lighten your load and provide useful perspective.

Things you can do:

Involve Your Partner or Family: Share tasks and ask for help when needed. For example, if mornings are chaotic, assign certain chores to your partner.

Connect with Other ADHD Parents: Join support groups or online communities where you can share tips, vent complaints, and find comfort from others who understand your experience.

Seek Professional Help: ADHD coaching or therapy can help you develop personalized techniques for handling both parenting and your own symptoms.

Don't forget that asking for help is a sign of strength, not weakness.

5. Be a good example of self-compassion.

Setting a positive example of self-compassion is one of the best things you can do for your kids. When they see you being honest about your problems and being kind to yourself, they will do the same.

Things you can do:

Say sorry and move on. If you lose your anger or forget something important, own up to it, say sorry, and resolve to do better next time.

Self-care means setting aside time for things that make you feel good, like going for a walk, writing in a book, or hanging out with friends. A parent who gets enough rest and stays calm is better at their job.

Such as:

When you say, "I'm sorry I yelled earlier. By telling your kids things like, "I was feeling overwhelmed, but I'm working on handling my feelings better," you show them that it's okay to mess up and that they can always grow.

Questions People Ask About Raising a Child with ADHD

"How do I deal with the guilt that comes from thinking I'm not doing enough?"

Remember that feeling guilty shows that you really care about your kids. Don't let it get you down; instead, use it to push yourself to keep trying. What matters most is your daily love and work for your family.

"What if my ADHD drives my kids crazy?"

ADHD can make it simple for people to misunderstand each other, but clear conversation can help clear things up. Talk to your kids about your problems in a way that is appropriate for their age and get them involved in finding answers. You could say something like, "I forget things sometimes, so let's work together to make reminders."

How having ADHD can help you be a better parent

ADHD makes things hard, but it also gives you the tools to be a wonderful parent:

Empathy: Because you are emotionally sensitive, you can connect deeply with your kids and understand how they feel.

Spontaneity: Your love of new things and being surprised can make magical, joyful times for your family.

Resilience: Dealing with your ADHD gives you the strength and imagination to get through tough times.

When you focus on these strengths, you'll see that ADHD doesn't make being a parent harder; instead, it makes it better.

Your action plan for being a parent

To do well as a father of a child with ADHD, follow these steps:

Release Perfection: Don't worry about perfect performance; instead, focus on relationship.

To stay organized, use visual plans, job chunking, and habit anchoring to settle into simple routines.

Celebrate Your Strengths: Be proud of your imagination, kindness, and ability to make people happy.

Ask for Help: Allow your partner, family, or a support group to help you and give you advice.

Self-compassion: Show your kids how to learn from their mistakes by doing it yourself.

How to Parent with Purpose

To thrive as a parent with ADHD, you can't get rid of problems. Instead, you have to accept yourself and use your unique skills to make your family a loving, helpful place.

You're not just getting by; you're teaching your kids to be strong and caring and to see the beauty in flaws. That's an amazing thing to leave behind.

SOCIAL SKILLS THAT WORK: USEFUL ADVICE FOR MAKING FRIENDS AND AVOIDING BEING ALONE

"I told myself for years that I didn't need a lot of friends." Still, I was worn out of being alone and thought it would be safer to stay away than to say or do something stupid.

A lot of women with ADHD find it easier to be alone than to deal with the challenges of social interactions. Socializing can be dangerous because people are afraid of making mistakes like cutting someone off, forgetting their name, or feeling like they are not being understood. I know what it's like to feel like you're not "good enough" to connect with someone or that your quirks will turn them off. I did learn one thing, though: a relationship isn't about being perfect, and social skills are just that—skills. You can learn them, practice them, and change them to fit your own skills.

Let's talk about how to improve your social skills so that you feel less alone and make links that feel real and important.

Why ADHD can make it hard to make friends

ADHD can make it harder to get along with other people. You may have trouble controlling your impulses, stopping others by mistake, or talking too much. If you're time-blind, you might be late to meetings, and if you forget things, you might miss parties or not return calls. When you add mental sensitivity to the mix, it's simple to see why interacting can be hard.

"People with ADHD often misinterpret social cues or feel hyper-aware of their mistakes, which can lead to withdrawing from social situations altogether," says Dr. Kathleen Nadeau, a specialist in ADHD and social skills.

There is positive news, though: these problems don't have to rule your social life. You can boost your confidence and feel less alone if you know your own unique social habits and use useful tactics.

Step 1: Change the way you think

Before you start talking about tips and tricks, you should think about the stories you might be telling yourself about making friends. "I'm too awkward to make friends" or "People don't want to connect with me" are two things you might be telling yourself. These thoughts put up walls that keep you from talking to other people.

Things you can do:

Challenge Negative Beliefs: When you feel like criticizing yourself, say something positive to yourself like, "I add value to conversations" or "Everyone makes social mistakes—it's part of being human."

Focus on Connection, Not Perfection: When you're mingling, the point isn't to be perfect; it's to connect with other people and enjoy the conversation.

This change in how people think sets the stage for real social growth.

Step 2: Get better at listening actively

Active listening is one of the best ways to connect with other people. People with ADHD often have trouble staying in the moment, especially when the talk isn't interesting right away. You might not fully listen because you are zoned out or making plans for what to say next.

Things you can do:

Pay attention to the speaker's body language and facial reactions to stay interested.

After someone talks, recap what they said to show that you heard what they had to say. For example, you could say, "It sounds like you had a great vacation!"

Before you answer, pause. Consider their words for a moment before responding.

Active listening not only makes your relationships stronger, but it also makes you feel less stressed out about whether you're saying the "right" thing.

Step 3: Set social goals that are attainable.

For someone with ADHD, the thought of making lots of friends can be too much. Focus on small, doable goals instead of trying to change everything all at once.

Things you can do:

Start Small: promise to have one important contact a week, like a coffee date, phone call, or going to an event in your area.

If getting in touch with someone seems hard, tell yourself you'll only spend five minutes texting or making plans. Beginning is often the hardest part.

Celebrate your progress: Be proud of your work, even if it seems small. With each step, you get closer to ending isolation.

For example, don't feel like you have to throw a big dinner party right away. Instead, invite one friend over for coffee.

Step 4: Use strategies that work for people with ADHD

People with ADHD don't necessarily have the same experience when they interact with others. Employ strategies that align with your brain's wiring.

Things you can do:

Plan Your Conversations Ahead of Time: If you're feeling worried about a social event, make a list of questions or topics you'd like to talk about. For instance, "What's the coolest thing you've done this month? can lead to interesting talks.

Use visual reminders: Keep important dates, such as birthdays, and notes from conversations, such as someone's favorite pastime, in your phone or calendar.

Find Low-Stress Social Settings: Instead of going to loud, busy places, choose places where you feel safe, like a quiet coffee shop or a casual meetup group.

These tips make hanging out with other people less stressful and more fun.

Step Five: Learn How to Get Over Making Social Mistakes

Whether you have ADHD or not, everyone makes mistakes with other people. The only difference is that ADHDers repeat the event and imagine the worst.

Things you can do:

Say sorry when you need to: If you cut someone off or forget something important, a simple, sincere apology can make things right. For instance, "I'm sorry I cut you off earlier; I was really interested in what you were saying."

Move on: Remind yourself that one awkward moment doesn't make the whole conversation bad. Most of the time, people are more willing to forgive than we think.

Use It as a Chance to Learn: Think about what went wrong and how you could handle it differently next time.

You should see social slip-ups as a normal part of the process and not as a reason to stay away from people.

Step 6: Make friends who will help you.

Spending time with people who don't understand or value your unique qualities can make you feel alone. Focus on making friends with people who like you just the way you are.

Things you can do:

Find communities of people who share your views: Join interest-based groups, ADHD support networks, or online boards to meet people who have been through the same things you have.

Choose Quality Over Quantity: A small group of close, helpful friends is better than a large group of strangers.

Be yourself: Show off your quirks. People who get you will enjoy your fun, energy, and innovation.

For example, if you love crafting, joining a local art class or an online group of crafters can help you make real, important connections.

Questions People Ask About Getting Better at Social Skills

"What if I feel bad talking to people?"

Start with easy things to do, like leaving a comment on a social media post or sending a quick text message that says, "Thinking of you." Small steps like these help you feel more confident over time.

"What should I do when I feel rejected?"

Keep in mind that rejection is a common occurrence in social interactions and does not imply a lack of personal worth. Pay attention to those who help you and ignore the rest.

Social skills can help people feel less alone.

You can make more relationships and have a more satisfying life when you learn useful social skills. People will gladly accept your efforts, even if they're not perfect.

Imagine being excited about lunch with friends who know and care about you or being able to easily start a conversation at a neighborhood event. These times don't just make you feel less alone; they also tell you that you're part of a lively, helpful society.

Your plan to improve your social skills.

Here is a step-by-step plan to help you feel less alone and more confident:

Change the way you think: connect with others instead of being perfect.

Active listening means being present and interested in what other people are saying.

Set small goals, like making a promise to talk to someone once a week.

Adopt strategies for ADHD: set alarms, plan ahead, and go to places with low stress.

Recover with grace: Move on after making a mistake.

Build a Supportive Circle: Spend time with people who love the things that make you special.

You are about to connect.

Being social doesn't mean changing who you are; it means finding real and powerful ways to connect with other people. You can spend less time alone and make important connections that make your life better with practice and care.

You're not going through this journey by yourself, and the way you connect with others is a gift. Let's do the first thing together.

Chapter 3: Making Connections That Matter

- "The strength of your connections lies not in how perfect you are but in how real and open you choose to be."
- The most important things to remember from Chapter 3 are:
- To improve your relationships, be clear and polite about what you need by using "I" words, active listening, and specific requests. This will help both people understand what you're saying.
- Finding Your ADHD Tribe: Look for friends and organizations that understand and support your ADHD, whether they are online, in real life, or through shared hobbies.
- ADHD in Love: Get through love relationships by showing empathy, having open talks about ADHD, and working together on ways to improve and understand each other.
- If you are a parent with ADHD, let go of the need to be perfect, find habits that work for you, and use your imagination and empathy to connect with your children.
- Social Skills That Work: To feel less alone, learn useful social skills, focus on real bonds, and learn how to calmly recover from mistakes.

Now that we've addressed your personal relationships, we can discuss work and school. In Chapter 4, you'll learn about tools and strategies that can help you deal with problems at work, make the most of your strengths, and use your ADHD to your job's benefit. Allow us to begin!

CHAPTER 4: EXCELLING AT WORK AND LEARNING

"Your ADHD isn't a roadblock—it's the key to unlocking unique strengths that can help you thrive in your career and education."

How to Pick a Job That Fits Your Strengths If You Have ADHD

"Imagine starting a new job with a lot of excitement and then quickly becoming overwhelmed and unmotivated after just a few weeks. It's not because you're untrained, but rather because your brain doesn't fit the job.

For ADHD women, life goals can be difficult to determine. You may do well in some roles but poorly in others, and you may wonder why something that looks "perfect on paper" doesn't feel right. The truth is that your ADHD changes how you do your job. However, knowing your strengths and weaknesses can help you find a job that fits and develops you.

Let's talk about how to find your unique strengths, stay away from undesirable career matches, and make a plan for a successful career.

Why ADHD Can Affect Job Options

People with ADHD need things that are interesting, new, and passionate. People with ADHD may struggle to stay interested in repetitive tasks, even if they're "stable" or "practical." According to Dr. Edward Hallowell, this is because your brain naturally gravitates toward tasks that spark curiosity and creativity.

This doesn't mean you can't succeed in structured settings, but you must be intentional about finding roles that match your style. If you don't, you might feel stuck, tired, or unappreciated.

<u>Step 1: Figure out what your ADHD strengths are.</u>

Making a career plan begins with defining your unique contributions. People with ADHD often have creative minds, excellent problem-solving skills, and lots of energy. But these qualities need the right setting to shine.

Ask Yourself:

What types of jobs make me lose sense of time?

Where have I excelled in the past, and why?

What comments do I regularly receive from others about my strengths?

Such as:

If you love thinking and coming up with big ideas, you might thrive in a creative or entrepreneurial job. If you take pleasure in assisting others and maintaining a high level of attention to detail, a hands-on profession such as teaching or healthcare could be a suitable fit for you.

<u>Step 2: Match Careers to Your Strengths</u>

Once you've found your strengths, the next step is finding jobs that align with them. Here's a breakdown of common ADHD strengths and possible job paths:

Creativity and Innovation: Careers in design, writing, advertising, or business enable you to think creatively and innovatively.

Problem-Solving: Roles in engineering, IT, or consulting provide chances to face challenges head-on.

Empathy and People Skills: Professions in counseling, social work, or healthcare let you connect deeply with others.

Energy and Enthusiasm: Jobs in sales, teaching, or event planning allow you to channel your energy into dynamic interactions.

Things you can do:

List the careers that align with your skills and study what a normal day looks like in each role. Look for clues about whether the surroundings and tasks would keep you interested.

<u>3. Don't fall into common career traps.</u>

Some jobs are ideal for people with ADHD because they use their strengths well, but others may be too much or too repetitive, or they require a lot of mental functioning skills.

Things to keep an eye out for:

Situations that are too rigid: Jobs that require strict obedience to rules or micromanagement can be stifling.

Minimal Creativity: If your job doesn't give you many chances to come up with new ideas or solve problems, you might get bored.

Too Many Details: Jobs that require you to pay close attention to details all the time, like accounting or data entry, can be emotionally draining.

You shouldn't avoid these jobs, but be aware of potential issues and modify them to your needs.

4. Make work systems that are beneficial for people with ADHD.

To be successful in your job for a long time, you need to set up processes that help your ADHD.

Things you can do:

Make use of visual tools. Task boards, planners, and calendars can assist you in maintaining focus and organization.

Break up big jobs into smaller, more manageable steps to keep from getting too stressed.

Use technology: To keep track of your chores and due dates, use apps like Trello, Notion, or Todoist.

Such as:

Using a CRM tool to keep track of leads and follow-ups can help you stay organized if you work in sales and things move quickly.

Step 5: Speak up for yourself

To succeed at work with ADHD, you may need to request accommodations or changes. This does not imply disclosing your condition to everyone, if you choose not to. It means figuring out what you need and how to get it.

Things you can do:

Focus on Solutions: Instead of seeing ADHD as a problem, talk about the things you do to do well. "I work best in short, focused bursts, so I use timers to get the most done," for example.

Set Limits: If you need to, ask for flexible dates or a quieter office.

Find help: Consult teachers or coworkers who understand your work style for advice.

Speaking up for yourself boosts self-esteem and allows you to grow.

Questions People Ask About ADHD and Jobs

"What should I do if I'm unsure?"

Start by looking around. Do things that interest you, like volunteer work, take classes, or follow pros around. Pay attention to what interests you and gets you excited.

"What if I feel trapped at my job?"

Find ways to make your job fit with what you're talented at. For instance, if you think your job is boring, ask for chances to work on artistic projects or solve issues. If you think it's impossible to make changes, you might want to make a long-term plan to move into a more satisfying job.

Having the right job can significantly transform your life.

If you have ADHD and find a job that fits your skills, work will no longer feel like a fight but like a chance to shine. Because you're doing work that fits with your natural skills, you'll feel more energized and motivated.

Imagine waking up with a sense of excitement, as your job both challenges you and honors the uniqueness of your brain. It's not a pipe dream—with the right plan, it's very possible.

Your career blueprint is your action plan.

Here is a step-by-step plan to help you pick a job that works with your ADHD:

Find Your Strengths: Think about what you like and what you're excelling at.

Explore Career Matches: Look into jobs that fit your natural skills.

Watch Out for Red Flags: Be wary of jobs that could drain or overload you.

Create Support Systems: To stay organized and get things done, use tools, habits, and plans.

You should advocate for yourself and request any accommodations that will help you succeed.

Your Job, Your Possibility

As a woman with ADHD, picking the right job isn't about fitting into someone else's mold. It's about building a career that excites and inspires you by accepting your unique strengths.

You possess a remarkable talent that awaits discovery. If you follow the right plan, your ADHD won't be a problem; instead, it will be your biggest strength. Let's plan your way to a career that makes you happy.

Focus Hacks for Work Success: How to Deal With Workplace Distractions

"You sit down at your desk ready to work on your list, but within minutes, your phone rings and your email comes in. Your mind then wanders to that random idea you had yesterday."When the day is over, you've worked hard but not gotten much done. Sense a pattern? "

People are distracted, and women with ADHD may feel like they're always getting in the way of their work. It can be challenging to maintain focus at work due to various factors such as an open office layout, excessive notifications, or persistent thoughts. But here's the positive news: with the right methods, you can control your focus and thrive in your work life.

Let's explore useful focus techniques designed especially for ADHD brains to help you overcome distractions and reach your maximum potential at work.

Why Distractions Hit Harder with ADHD

People with ADHD naturally crave new experiences and excitement. This makes boring or repetitive jobs unbearable. This, along with impaired brain function, explains why it can be extremely challenging to maintain focus.

A well-known ADHD researcher, Dr. Russell Barkley, says, "The ADHD brain struggles with self-regulation, which includes the ability to resist distractions and maintain focus on less stimulating tasks." But that doesn't mean it's impossible to focus—it just needs a different method.

Step 1: Figure out what's getting in the way.

To get past distractions, you must first figure out what makes you lose focus. Distractions can come from the outside, like noisy coworkers or messages, or from the inside, like racing thoughts or being tired.

Things you can do:

Keep track of your triggers. For one day, pay attention to when and why you lose focus. Do emails get in the way? Do you look through social media when you're bored?

Separate Internal and External Distractions: Figuring out whether the problem is with your surroundings or your way of thinking helps you find the right answers.

If your coworkers' loud talks are getting in the way of your work, you'll need something outside of work to help, like noise-canceling headphones. Brain dumps and awareness can help if your own thoughts are making you feel bad.

Step 2: Use Time Blocking for Structured Focus

Time blocking is one of the most effective focus tools for ADHD brains because it provides a clear plan for your day while allowing freedom.

How It Works:

Set aside time each day for specific tasks. Set the time, for example, to 9:00–10:00 a.m. for emails and from 10 to 11 a.m. for a big job.

Take breaks to avoid burnout and to replenish your energy.

Things you can do:

Start with Short Blocks: If you find it challenging to concentrate for long amounts of time, try starting with 25-minute blocks followed by a 5-minute break. We also refer to this as the Pomodoro Technique.

Plan Your Days: Do jobs that require a lot of concentration when you're most effective, like in the morning, afternoon, or evening.

Time blocking is beneficial for people with ADHD because it gives them order without making them feel stuck.

Step 3: Make sure there are no distractions around.

Your setting has a big impact on how well you can concentrate. A place that is suitable for people with ADHD keeps outside distractions to a minimum and encourages focus.

Things you can do:

Clear off your desk: Only keep the things you need close to your work area to avoid visible distractions.

Use headphones. White noise apps or headphones with noise-blocking capabilities can effectively block out nearby conversations.

Limit digital interruptions: Turn off phone and computer alerts that aren't necessary. Use apps like Freedom or Focus@Will to block sites that are annoying at work.

Picture yourself sitting down to work with a clean desk, no messages, and soothing music playing in the background. It's easier to stay focused when there aren't many other things going on.

Step 4: Break Tasks into Bite-Sized Steps

Big jobs can feel overwhelming, leading to delay or mental paralysis. Breaking them into smaller, doable steps makes them more manageable and less scary.

Things you can do:

Make a list of all the things you need to do to finish a job. Instead of "Write Report," divide it into "Outline Sections," "Draft Introduction," and "Proofread."

Mark your progress by crossing off each step as you finish it. This makes you feel satisfied about what you've done and keeps you driven.

If you're getting ready for a show, don't try to finish the whole deck at once; instead, start with one slide.

Step 5: Use stimulation and movement

People with ADHD often struggle with staying still for extended periods of time. Moving around or doing something physical during the workday can help you stay focused.

Things you can do:

Take Breaks to Move: Stand up, stretch, or go for a short walk during your breaks.

Strategically fidget: Keep a stress ball or other fidget toy at your desk to keep your mind off of things that are bothering you.

For instance, set a timer for 45 minutes of work and then take a 5-minute walk around the office. This clears your thoughts and keeps you from getting tired.

Step 6: Put your responsibilities on someone else.

Having someone or something hold you responsible can really help you stay on track.
Things you can do:
Pair up with a friend or coworker and check in on each other's progress.

Set dates. Even if you set them for yourself, deadlines give people with ADHD a sense of urgency that they love.

Use tools. Apps like Asana and Trello can help you keep track of your work and see how far you've come.

For example, tell a coworker, "I'll send you the draft by 3 p.m." This makes you less likely to put things off.

Questions People Ask About Being Focused at Work

"What if my stress level remains high?"

It's okay to step back and start over. Focus on just one job at a time, and tell yourself that progress, not perfection, is the goal.

"What should I do when my coworkers talk over me?"

Be kind but strong when setting limits. You could say something like, "I'm busy right now. Can we catch up later?""

How will these hacks change the way you work?

When you use these hacks to focus, work is less about fighting off distractions and more about using your skills. It will be easier for you to get things done, meet goals, and feel satisfied at the end of the day instead of angry.

You could finish a job early because you stuck to the plan, or you could leave the office with a clear head and be ready to enjoy the evening. These goals aren't just dreams; they're completely doable with the right tools and attitude.

Your Action Plan for Focus Hacks

Here are some steps you can take to improve your focus at work:

Find Distractions: Write down what takes your mind away and deal with those things.

Set up time blocks with breaks throughout the day.

Optimize Your Environment: Clear off your desk and cut down on digital interruptions as much as possible.

Break tasks down: Break up big jobs into small steps that you can do.

Move around: To stay focused, take activity breaks or use fidget toys.

Use deadlines, tools, or partners to keep yourself on track. This is called externalizing accountability.

How You Can Master Focus

Getting past distractions doesn't mean changing who you are; it means setting up a workspace and pattern that works for your ADHD brain. These tips will not only help you get more done, but they will also help you feel better about your job and enjoy it again.

Let's make it happen! You have everything you need to do well.

TIME MASTERY MADE EASY: KEEPING TRACK OF YOUR SCHEDULE WITHOUT GETTING TOO STRESSED OUT

"It's 9 a.m., and you already feel overwhelmed." You've promised yourself to finish your most important tasks today, but your phone's to-do list is insane. Sense a pattern?"

For women with ADHD, keeping track of time can be like juggling sand—no matter how hard you try, it just slips out of your hands. Sometimes it seems impossible to organize your time because you miss meetings, forget deadlines, and feel like you'll never catch up. But here's the truth: being in charge of your time doesn't mean doing more. It means doing what works for you.

Let's look at some easy, ADHD-friendly ways to keep track of your plan without getting stressed out or overwhelmed.

Why Time Feels Slippery with ADHD

People with ADHD often have trouble telling time. People tend to live in the "now" or the "not now," where things that aren't happening right now don't seem real. It's challenging to set priorities, guess how long things will take, or make plans ahead of time when this happens.

A well-known ADHD researcher, Dr. Russell Barkley, says, "The ADHD brain has trouble thinking about the future, which makes it harder to organize and sequence tasks." In short, it's not laziness; it's a neurological problem. With the right tools and strategies, you can overcome this issue and manage your time.

Step 1: Embrace the Power of Visual Planning

People with ADHD tend to forget things that are out of sight, so it's important to keep your plan obvious and real. Visual planning tools help you stay on track and keep your mind clear of all the things you need to remember.

Things you can do:

Use a big schedule: Clearly display your monthly or weekly schedule. Use color-coded markers to make it simple to keep track of your meetings, due dates, and chores.

Use a time-blocking planner to set aside specific chunks of time for meetings, chores, and self-care. Seeing a picture of your day helps you concentrate on what's coming up.

Imagine walking into your kitchen and seeing a vibrantly colored calendar on the wall. It tells you right away what's important today without you having to dig through your phone or memory.

Step 2: Divide your day into chunks that you can handle.

While completing all the tasks in one day can be challenging, breaking them up into smaller ones makes them easier to manage.

Things you can do:

Start with Three Priorities: Each day, pick just three important things to work on. Having a short list of things to do helps you feel like you've accomplished something.

Don't add a task to your list if you can complete it in less than two minutes. Instead, do it right away. These little wins make room in your mind for more important things.

One way to break up the sentence "clean the house" is to write it as "tidy the living room" or "load the dishwasher." Each small step gets you closer to your goal.

Step 3: Make sure your schedule has breaks.

People with ADHD often have trouble switching between tasks, which can make them put things off or feel stuck. Adding transition time to your schedule can help with these changes.

Things you can do:

Set Timer Alerts: A timer can let you know when to finish one task and get ready for the next.

Plan for buffer time: Give yourself 10–15 minutes to clear your mind and get back to work between meetings or tasks.

Setting a timer for 10 minutes early to go over your notes and mentally switch gears can help you finish a report before a Zoom call.

4. Use tools that are beneficial for people with ADHD.

Using the right tools can optimize your time.

Things you can do:

Use digital calendars. Apps like Google Calendar and Outlook let you make events that happen again and again and share your plans across all of your devices.

Use task management apps. Todoist, Asana, and Trello are just a few examples. These apps make it easy to visualize and prioritize tasks.

Try Visual Timers: A timer that counts down or changes colors, like the Time Timer, can help you keep track of time.

For instance, program your phone to remind you to check your calendar every morning. This small habit helps you stick to your plans.

Step 5: Plan based on how much energy you have.

People with ADHD experience fluctuations in their brain activity throughout the day. Planning your tasks around your natural energy highs and lows helps you work smarter, not harder.

Things you can do:

Tackle High-Energy Tasks First: Schedule demanding or creative tasks during your most alert times (e.g., morning or mid-afternoon).

Save Low-Energy Tasks for Later: Use quieter times for routine tasks like answering emails or sorting paperwork.

Example: If your brain feels sharpest in the morning, commit that time to thinking or problem-solving. Use the afternoon for simpler jobs that don't require as much attention.

Step 6: Build flexibility into your day.

Rigid plans rarely work for ADHD brains because life is uncertain. Creating a flexible framework helps you to change without feeling like you've failed.

Things you can do:

Plan "Catch-Up" Time: Give yourself 30 minutes every day to do anything you didn't get to earlier.

Plan for the Unexpected: Add extra time to your plan in case something comes up.

Say a meeting lasts longer than planned. Take advantage of the extra time to finish the delayed task. This keeps one interruption from ruining your whole day.

Questions People Ask About Managing Their Time

"What if I do not meet the due date?"

Anyone can have it, even those without ADHD. Rather than dwelling on the issue, consider solutions: engage with the impacted individual, modify your strategy, and commit to avoiding the same mistake in the future.

"How do I deal with putting things off?"

Start out small. Stick with a job for five minutes at a time. That's often enough to get past the initial reluctance and gain momentum.

How mastering time changes your day

Everything else will work out when you take charge of your time. You can handle deadlines and chores without being too scary, and at the end of the day you feel like you accomplished something instead of being frustrated.

Imagine knowing your strategy and when to execute it. The time and energy you save with these tips will help you be more productive and enjoy life.

Your Action Plan for Mastering Time

Here are some steps you can take to make your plan easier:

Visualize your plans: Use diaries and calendars to keep track of your time.

Break Up Tasks: Make your day into small pieces that you can handle.

Allow time to move your attention from one job to the next.

Use Tools: To stay organized, use apps, timers, and notes.

Align with Your Energy Levels: Plan your work around the times you're most effective.

Be adaptable: Don't feel guilty about altering your plans when life presents unexpected challenges.

How You Can Master Time

Take charge of your time by creating your own schedule. With these tips, you can confidently handle your schedule, feel less stressed, and concentrate on what's important.

You can utilize your time wisely as it holds significant value. Let's do the first thing together.

HOW CAN WE HELP STUDENTS WITH ADHD LEARN IN A WAY THAT REALLY WORKS?

"You're ready to pay attention in class, but the teacher's words mix up, your mind wanders to unrelated things, and you're scrambling to catch up before you know it." Do you know what this is?"

It can be challenging for a woman with ADHD to find her way around the classroom. The standard learning setting doesn't always work well for people with ADHD, whether they are students going back to school or professionals in training. However, there is good news: you're not alone, and there are strategies you can implement to excel in school.

Let's look at some ADHD-friendly learning methods that will help you focus, understand, and succeed in school.

Why ADHD makes traditional learning hard

ADHD affects the part of your brain that helps you focus, organize, and keep track of time. Children with ADHD often struggle with traditional classes that rely on passive listening, strict scheduling, and one-way lessons, as their brains require stimulation, movement, and exposure to new concepts.

An expert on ADHD, Dr. Thomas E. Brown, says, "Students with ADHD are not less smart; they just process and interact with information differently." Knowing these differences is important for finding solutions that work for you.

Step 1: Split lectures into chunks that you can handle.

Sitting through a long lesson can feel difficult when your attention starts to waver after

15 minutes. Breaking the information into smaller, digestible pieces can make it easier to stay focused.

Things you can do:

Take Notes in Sections: Divide your page into small parts and focus on recording the main points for each section of the lesson.

Use Keywords and Symbols: Instead of writing full lines, jot down keywords, phrases, or symbols that help you remember key ideas.

Pause and Reflect: After every 15–20 minutes of teaching, take a quick moment to review what you've learned in your own words.

For instance, if your professor is discussing a historical event, record the "cause" and "effect," then use lines or diagrams to illustrate the connection between the two.

Step 2: Use more than one sense to learn

Using multiple senses while learning can improve memory because people with ADHD require constant stimulation.

Things you can do:

Highlight Important Points: To draw attention to important parts of your readings or notes, use colored highlighters or sticky notes.

Move around: If possible, pace or stand while reviewing the information. You can stay focused even if you just tap your foot or use a fidget tool.

Utilize audiovisual resources: Watch videos, listen to recorded classes, or use apps that let you connect with your lessons.

For example, if you are learning anatomy, you can look at and interact with 3D models or apps that show the human body.

Step 3: Ask for classroom modifications

Many schools provide ADHD accommodations, but you may need to request them.

Things you can do:

Ask for More Time: If timed tests stress you out, ask for more time to finish your tests.

Sit strategically: Choose a seat close to the front to maintain focus on the teacher and prevent distractions.

Use recorders: If taking notes is challenging for you, ask to have classes recorded so you can listen to them again later.

For example, a college student with ADHD might ask to use a laptop to take notes, even if the class doesn't allow them. Their ability to keep up can improve with this small change.

Step 4: Create a study schedule.

ADHDers need structure to study, but not rigidity. You can stay on track by making a plan that is flexible and full of different things.

Things you can do:

Time yourself: Set a timer for 25 to 30 minutes of serious study, and then take a 5-minute break. This is called the Pomodoro Technique.

Study in Sprints: Break your study sessions into focused sprints, with defined goals for each session.

Change Topics or Subjects: Changing topics or subjects keeps your brain active and stops you from getting bored.

For example, if you're studying for tests, go over your class notes for 30 minutes and then do problem sets for another 30 minutes.

Step 5: Work together and connect

It's not necessary to learn by yourself. Working with friends or joining study groups can hold you accountable and make the process more fun.

Things you can do:

Create a Study Group: Work with a friend to go over material, share notes, and test each other.

If you need more information or explanation, don't be afraid to ask your teacher.

Teach What You Learn: Teaching others about ideas helps you understand them better.

For example, have your class join an online website or group chat where they can share their ideas, ask questions, and help each other.

Step 6: Don't seek perfection, but focus on progress.

There is a lot of focus on grades and behavior in school, which can be too much for someone with ADHD. Focusing on growth instead of perfection can help you stay focused and less stressed.

Things you can do:

Celebrate Small Wins: See each task or quiz you finish as a step toward your goals.

Focus on Growth: Don't try to get a perfect score; instead, work on getting smarter and better at what you do.

Treat yourself with kindness. Remember that learning takes time and that mistakes are a normal part of the process.

If you didn't do well on a test, don't think about the score too much. Instead, think about what you can do better on the next test.

How to talk to kids about ADHD in the classroom

"What if I fall behind in school?"

Get in touch with your teacher or assistant right away. If you're persistent and work hard, most teachers will help.

"How can I stay motivated when class is boring?"

One small goal could be to take excellent notes for the next 10 minutes. Another idea is to give yourself a treat after class. Connect the information to things you're interested in to make it more interesting.

How strategies for ADHD change the way we learn

Using techniques that work with ADHD transforms the classroom from a battleground to a place where people can learn and grow. It will be straightforward for you to stay interested, understand the information, and show that you can learn.

Imagine being sure of yourself when you go to class because you know you have tools to help you stay focused and learn. In addition to getting by, these tips will help you excel as you learn.

Your Action Plan for the Classroom

Here are the steps you need to take to do well in school:

Break lectures up into smaller chunks and use buzzwords or symbols to make notes.

Engage Your Senses: To learn better, use pictures, movement, and tools that you can connect with.

Request some accommodations: Ask for changes that will help you learn.

Set up a study routine. To stay on track, use clocks, sprints, and topic changes.

Work together: To get help, pair up with classmates or join a study group.

Focus on Progress: Be proud of how much you've grown and see learning as a journey.

How do you want to learn?

You can do well in school even if you have ADHD. You can enjoy school and do well when you use brain-friendly methods.

You are strong, skilled, and ready to face obstacles. This is the moment to utilize your ADHD to your advantage in the classroom.

THE BEST TOOLS AND APPS FOR MANAGING ADHD ARE THOSE THAT USE TECHNOLOGY.

What if you have a multitude of tasks on your mind, such as work-related tasks, your child's upcoming dentist appointment, and an email you've forgotten to send? Your planner isn't helping you with any of it. Technology has become your greatest ally in managing the chaos.

The right apps and tools can make all the difference for people with ADHD. Technology doesn't just help you remember things; it also speeds up your day, keeps you organized, and even helps you relax. Let's talk about how to use technology in ways that work for your brain and change the way you go about your daily life.

The impact of technology on individuals with ADHD has been significant.

People with ADHD require organization and reminders, but manually setting up and maintaining these processes can be challenging. Technology fills in this gap by giving you quick, flexible options that fit your needs. A well-known expert on ADHD, Dr. Edward Hallowell, says, "Externalizing organization is the key to managing ADHD." The best way to do that is through technology.

Tech tools, like timers and focus aids, can make difficult chores easier and help you stay on track.

Step 1: Use calendar apps to keep track of your time.

People with ADHD often have trouble keeping track of their schedules, due dates, and to-do lists. Calendar apps let you keep track of your time in one place and in a clear way.

Things you can do:

Use color coding: To clearly separate tasks based on importance, give different colors to different groups, such as blue for work and green for personal chores.

Set Reminders: To remind yourself, set alerts for 15 to 30 minutes before meetings or due dates.

Use apps like Google Calendar or Apple Calendar that sync your phone, tablet, and computer so that everything stays in sync.

If you opened your calendar in the morning and saw a color-coded plan of your day, with gentle notes that show up when you need them, that would be amazing.

Set up your tasks with to-do list apps (Step 2).

Digital task management apps let you plan, prioritize, and take on jobs one step at a time. Traditional to-do lists can get big too fast.

Things you can do:

Use subtasks to break up big jobs into smaller steps that you can handle. You can do this in apps like Todoist and Microsoft To Do.

Labels can help you set priorities. Sort tasks by urgency to focus on what's most important.

Set Recurring Reminders: Setting up automatic reminders for things like paying bills or doing your weekly jobs is a beneficial idea.

Instead of looking at a long list of tasks like "clean the house," you break them down into smaller ones like "vacuum the living room" and "fold laundry." Each step you finish makes you feel like you're making progress, which is great.

Step 3: Use tools for productivity to stay on track.

Distractions can make it challenging for people with ADHD to focus, but work apps can help you stay on task and cut down on interruptions.

Things you can do:

Block Distractions: Apps such as Freedom and Focus Will filter distracting websites and create environments conducive to concentration.

Use Timers: To try the Pomodoro Technique, use apps like Forest that tell you to work in short bursts and then take breaks.

Track Your Time: Toggl and other apps allow you to monitor your time, enabling you to identify patterns and modify your habits.

Let's say you set a timer for 25 minutes on Forest and work while watching a fake tree grow. You stay focused because it makes you pleased to see your tree grow.

Step 4: Use digital tools to keep track of your notes and ideas.

It's annoying to forget things like thoughts or important notes. Digital note-taking apps keep your ideas close at all times.

Things you can do:

Bring all of your notes together: Use Evernote or OneNote to keep all of your notes, pictures, and links in one place.

With voice-to-text apps like Otter.ai, you can dictate notes when typing is too slow or boring.

Digital tools make it simple to quickly look for old notes or ideas without having to read through papers.

While stuck in traffic, you recall an idea for a project. You record it right away with a voice-to-text app and then move it to your project folder.

Step 5: Use relaxation apps to calm down.

Taking care of ADHD isn't just about getting things done; it's also about finding calm times during a busy day. Apps for mindfulness and relaxing can help you feel less stressed and concentrate better.

Things you can do:

Guided meditation can help you relax. Apps like Headspace and Calm have short, easy-to-use lessons designed for people who are new to meditation.

Use breathing tools. Apps like Breathe+ offer guided breathing exercises that can help you relax.

Use white noise: Play soothing background sounds while working or resting with apps like Noisli.

For example, you use a breathing app for five minutes after a busy morning. The guided exercise clears your mind, which makes it easier to move on to the next job.

Step 6: Use habit-building apps to keep track of your progress.

It can be hard to form habits when you have ADHD, but apps that track them can help you stay focused and steady.

Things you can do:

Start Small: To make building habits more fun, use apps like Habitica that give you points for finishing chores.

See Your Progress: Apps like Streaks let you see your progress over time, which encourages you to keep going.

Set Your Own Goals: You can change the things that your habit tracker tracks, like how often you drink water or how often you write in your notebook.

Say you want to walk for 10 minutes every day. The app's streak grows every time you finish something, giving you a dopamine boost that makes you more likely to keep going.

Questions People Ask About Using Technology to Help with ADHD

"What if using too many apps causes me to feel stressed?"

Start out small. Select a few tools to help you solve your most pressing issues, then add more as needed.

"How am I going to remember to use the applications?"

You can set notes or make the tools a part of your daily life. For instance, review your morning to-do list while drinking coffee.

Technology transforms the management of ADHD.

If used correctly, technology can be a useful tool for managing ADHD. It takes the pressure off of the things and processes in your brain that you find hard, giving you more mental energy for growth, creativity, and attention.

With the help of tools designed specifically for you, imagine starting the day with a clear plan, maintaining focus during well-timed sprints, and feeling proud of what you've accomplished by the end of the day. It's not only possible; it's close at hand.

What is your plan for using technology?

Here are the steps to use technology to manage ADHD:

- Master Scheduling: Use calendar tools to keep track of chores and meetings.
- Sort Tasks: To-do list apps can help you set priorities and break jobs down into smaller steps.
- Focus: To stay on task, block out distractions with efficiency tools and work in short bursts.
- Gather ideas: Use digital tools that sync across devices to keep all of your notes in one place.
- Relax and recharge: To relieve stress, add mindfulness tools to your daily life.
- Record Your Habits: To stay steady and enjoy your growth, use apps that help you form new habits.

How You Want to Use Technology

Although technology isn't a panacea for everyone, with the right tools, it can function as a customized personal assistant for your ADHD brain. Try new things, change them around, and see what works best for you.

You are empowered to make things clear and organized out of chaos and confusion. Let's use the tools that allow us to do it.

Chapter 4: Doing Great at Work and School

The most important things to remember from Chapter 4 are:

- Career Blueprint for People with ADHD: Figure out what you're talented at and pick a job that uses your imagination, energy, and ability to solve problems. Stay away from jobs that are too rigid or repetitive because they will wear you down.
- Focus Hacks for Work Success: To stay busy and on task, use time-blocking, break jobs down into smaller steps, and make sure you don't have any distractions around.
- Time Mastery Made Easy: Use visual tools, planned habits, and the freedom to deal with unexpected problems without feeling too stressed to keep track of your schedule.
- ADHD students can learn better by breaking up lessons, using multiple senses, and asking for customized changes.
- Technology: To make your day easier and help you stay on track, use apps for organizing, managing tasks, focusing, being aware, and keeping track of your habits.

You need to change yourself now that you have the tools to succeed at work and school. In Chapter 5, you'll learn how to make your mind and body work together in balance, boost your confidence, and make a self-care plan that will help you do well. Let's move forward together!

CHAPTER 5:
TRANSFORMING YOUR LIFE

*"Growth happens when you take what you've
learned and use it to create a life you love."*

How to Make an ADHD Toolkit: The Essentials You Need to Succeed

"Did you know that Simone Biles, the most decorated gymnast of all time, openly credits managing her ADHD as part of her journey to success? She calls her ADHD strategies her 'secret weapon,' helping her focus, stay resilient, and thrive under pressure."

As soon as I heard Simone Biles talk about her ADHD, I felt like I knew her. There was someone at the top of her field dealing with the same problems I did every day. It helped me remember that getting rid of ADHD isn't the key to success; it's learning how to work with it. You can build your own ADHD toolkit to help you do well in life, just like Simone has a set of tools that help her do well in gymnastics.

Let's talk about the essentials for creating your own toolkit to stay organized, take charge, and succeed in all areas of life.

How and why do you need an ADHD toolkit?

Managing time, staying focused, dealing with feelings, and keeping track of tasks can feel like a lot of things to do when you have ADHD. A well-made toolkit is more than just a collection of techniques; it's your unique roadmap for navigating life with ADHD.

An expert on ADHD, Dr. Ned Hallowell, says, "Tools give you the structure that ADHD brains need but find hard to make on their own." They make sense out of chaos.

Your ADHD toolbox is what you use to deal with problems and make your skills shine.

Step 1: Get your main tools ready.

Planning, focusing, and managing time are three of the most common problems that people with ADHD face. Every backpack should have these basic tools.

Things you can do:

Planner or Calendar: Whether it's a digital app like Google Calendar or a paper planner with color-coded parts, choose a method that works for you.

Use Todoist or Trello as a task manager to keep track of your work.

Timers: A visual timer, like Time Timer, or an app with a countdown feature can help you keep track of your focus times and move from one job to the next.

Imagine starting the day by going over your calendar and to-do list. You could use a timer to keep you on track, and as the day ends, crossing things off your list would make you feel satisfied about what you've done.

Step 2: Add tools to help you control your emotions

Especially for women with ADHD, controlling your feelings can be one of the hardest things about having the disorder. Using tools to control your emotions can help you deal with worry, being sensitive to rejection, and feeling overwhelmed.

Things you can do:

Journaling App or Notebook: Writing down your feelings and thoughts can help you understand them better and calm down.

Meditation and deep breathing apps, such as Calm and Headspace, can help you deal with stress by leading you through routines and videos.

Tools for Relieving Worry: For times when you feel overwhelmed, keep a worry ball, a fidget toy, or even a weighted blanket on hand.

For example, you write down how you feel about a frustrating work call and then do a short meditation on your app. This straightforward process can help you reset and get back on track.

Step 3: Purchase some organizers for your personal use.

Most of the time, people with ADHD lose things, forget meetings, or feel too cluttered. Organizational systems are important for making things clear and simple to understand.

Things you can do:

Home Command Center: Set aside a place for important things like wallets, keys, and papers so you don't have to waste time looking for them.

Label Everything: Put labels on storage boxes, shelves, and drawers to make it easier to find things and put them back where they belong.

Set a Weekly Reset Routine: To keep things in order, clean up and organize your space for 30 minutes every week.

Say you put your mail and keys in a box next to your front door. Every Friday, you sort the basket and put everything back where it belongs. This small habit keeps things from getting too messy.

Step 4: Add apps that are beneficial for people with ADHD

Technology can make it easier to deal with ADHD. Having the right tools can make your life easier and help you stay on track.

Things you can do:

Focus Apps: To stay on task while you work or study, use apps like Forest or Focus Will.

Stick to your habits by using apps like Habitica that make it enjoyable and rewarding to do so.

Taking digital notes: Evernote or OneNote can consolidate all your notes and thoughts into a single location.

For example, make a habit tracker to help you stick to new habits, like exercise or drinking water. Every streak is like a small win.

Step 5: Add tools for time management and self-care

Having ADHD isn't just about getting things done; it's also about taking care of your physical and mental health. For long-term success, you need tools for self-care and managing your energy.

Things you can do:

Help with Sleep: Apps like Sleep Cycle keep track of how you sleep and can help you form better sleep habits.

Food Reminders: Set alarms to help you remember to eat healthy meals on a regular basis.

Tools for Exercise: To add movement to your habit, keep workout gear or an app like MyFitnessPal on hand.

Example: To get a better night's sleep, set an alarm for the evening to do something relaxing, like reading or stretching.

Questions People Often Ask About ADHD Toolkits

"What if the tool doesn't work when I try it?"

That is totally normal. Consider your toolkit as a dynamic resource that you can utilize and modify as necessary. It's fine if what works for someone else doesn't work for you.

"How can I consistently remember to use my tools?"

Start out small. First practice one or two tools, then incorporate them into your routine. As an example, check your notebook every morning while you drink your coffee.

How can an ADHD toolkit transform your life?

A well-designed ADHD toolkit empowers you to take charge, solve problems, and succeed. Imagine having a way to stay organized, keep your energy up, and control your feelings without having to deal with stress all the time.

Your toolbox is more than just a bunch of things; it shows how much you care about yourself and your growth. If you have the right tools, you're not just getting by; you're flourishing.

Your Action Plan for the ADHD Toolkit

Here's how to make your own set of tools for ADHD:

Start with Core Tools. To plan your day, pick a planner, a task manager, and a timer.

Add Tools for Emotional Regulation: Write in a journal, use mindfulness apps, or buy things that help you relax.

Set up systems for organization. For example, use signs, a home command center, and a weekly restart.

Use technology: Add apps that help you concentrate, keep track of your habits, and take notes.

Include self-care tools: To keep your energy up, put sleep, food, and exercise at the top of your list.

Your Success, Your Tools

You can't just control your ADHD symptoms when you make your tools. It's also about making your life work for you. You can take over the world with your tools, just like Simone Biles does with her methods in gymnastics.

With your strength and determination, no one can stop you with the right tools.

MIND AND BODY IN HARMONY: KEEPING YOUR MENTAL AND PHYSICAL HEALTH IN CHECK

"One of the best athletes of all time, Serena Williams, has talked a lot about how important it is to keep your mental and physical health in balance." What was her message? Your body and mind work together; when one is healthy, the other does too.

When Serena first talked about this, it made me realize how far away I'd been from my body. So focused on controlling my mind's chaos, I neglected its feeders. Sense a pattern? It's normal for women with ADHD to feel this way. Keeping yourself mentally and emotionally busy can make it easy to neglect your health.

However, there is a strong connection between your mental and physical health. One gets better when you take care of the other. Let's look at some ways you can harmonize your mind and body to live a healthy, energizing life.

Mind-body balance is important for people with ADHD.

ADHD affects your entire body, not just your brain. The effects of ADHD can be significant, ranging from difficulty sleeping to health problems caused by stress to mental tiredness. Finding a balance between your mental and physical health isn't just about feeling good; it's also about giving your brain the best conditions to grow.

"Exercise is like medicine for ADHD," says Dr. John Ratey, author of Spark: The Revolutionary New Science of Exercise and the Brain. It boosts happiness, attention, and mental clarity by affecting the same neurotransmitters that medications do. This shows how important it is to include physical health in your mental health plan.

Step 1: Start with Small, Sustainable Changes

The idea of overhauling your lifestyle can feel overwhelming, so start small. Small, consistent changes lead to lasting results.

Things you can do:

Begin with Movement: Incorporate small bursts of exercise into your day, like a 10-minute walk or stretching practice.

Prioritize Sleep: Set a regular bedtime and build a calming pre-sleep practice, like reading or meditating.

Drink water and eat healthy food. Keep a water bottle close by and try to eat or snack on one healthy thing every day.

Instead of sticking to a tough workout plan, try going for a daily 15-minute walk around your neighborhood. This small habit can help make bigger changes possible.

Step 2: Move around to clear your mind.

For people with ADHD, exercise isn't just a way to stay fit; it's also a way to control their feelings, focus better, and feel less stressed. Movement makes the brain chemicals dopamine and norepinephrine work better, which helps you stay awake and driven.

Things you can do:

Do things you enjoy. For example, gardening, dancing, swimming, yoga, or even swimming can help you work out and relax at the same time.

Engage in physical activity, such as walking while listening to a podcast or pacing while brainstorming ideas.

Move around as a way to reset. If you feel stuck or stressed, do some jumping jacks or stretch for a short time.

Let's say you're having trouble focusing on a report. You feel clearer and more energized when you get back to your desk after 10 minutes of walking and deep breathing.

Step 3: Start practicing mindfulness

The key to mindfulness is being aware of your thoughts without judging them. If you have ADHD, this practice can help you control your mental responses and feel less overwhelmed.

Things you can do:

Take it gently at first. Do 3–5 minutes of focused breathing every day to start.

Use guided tools. Apps like Calm and Insight Timer have meditations that are simple for beginners to do.

You can use mindfulness in everyday activities like eating, walking, or even washing dishes by focusing on the movements and feelings.

Instead of looking through your phone during lunch, take a moment to enjoy the tastes and textures of your food. Doing this simple thing can help you stay in the present.

Step 4: Take care of yourself to build emotional strength.

Having emotional resilience, or the ability to get back on your feet after a setback, is essential for handling ADHD. Self-care activities are beneficial for your mental health and make it easier for you to deal with worry.

Things you can do:

Make a self-care routine: Set aside time each week to do things that make you feel good, like writing in a notebook, drawing, or taking a bath.

Write down three things you're thankful for every day to shift your attention to the good in your life.

Set Limits: Learn to say "no" to commitments that drain your energy. This will make room for the things that really matter.

You light a candle, play soothing music, and write in your journal for 20 minutes every Sunday night about the coming week. This ritual helps you get ready and stay focused.

Step 5: Deal with stress before it gets worse

There will always be worry, but too much of it can be detrimental for your body and mind. Having go-to ways to deal with worry keeps it from taking over your life.

Things you can do:

How to Ground Yourself: If you feel anxious, try grounding techniques like the 5-4-3-2-1 method, which focuses on your feelings.

Schedule Breaks: Include breaks in your day to prevent burnout.

Reach Out for Support: Share your thoughts with a trusted friend, doctor, or support group.

Say you call a close friend after a rough day at work to talk about how you felt. Sharing your thoughts makes you feel better and helps you see things in a new way.

Questions People Ask About Mind-Body Balance

"What if I don't have time to work out or take care of myself?"

Start out small. Even five minutes of movement or awareness can make a difference. Remember, it's about progress, not perfection.

"How can I maintain these habits?"

Use notes, like phone alerts or visual cues, to adopt these habits into your daily routine. Pair new habits with old ones, like stretching while waiting for your coffee to brew.

How Mind-Body Harmony Transforms Your Life

When your mind and body are in balance, you build a basis for growth, resilience, and joy. Imagine being full of energy instead of tiredness, focused instead of scattered, and calm instead of stressed. Not only does this balance make your health better, it also changes how you live your whole life.

Imagine that you wake up feeling comfortable and refreshed. Moving around eliminates morning sluggishness, and your mind is clear and focused from the start. Finally, you've achieved your goals and taken care of yourself.

Your action plan for mind and body.

To get your mind and body to work together, do the following:

Start small. Make small habits easier to keep up, like going for short walks, drinking enough water, and having a relaxing routine before bed.

Move with Purpose: Exercise can help you reset your attention and deal with stress.

Mindfulness: Do some straightforward tasks to improve your awareness every day.

Put self-care first: schedule time for things that make you feel positive and give you ideas.

Deal with stress: Find ways to calm yourself and ask for help when you need it.

The way to balance yourself

In mental and physical health, balance is more important than perfection. You can make your life feel strong, energized, and at peace by taking small, deliberate steps.

You already have everything you need to do well. Let's move forward toward a life that is balanced and peaceful.

GETTING OVER **ADHD** WITH SELF-CONFIDENCE INVOLVES BOOSTING SELF-ESTEEM AND FAITH IN ONESELF.

"Michael Phelps, the most decorated Olympian of all time, has openly shared how his ADHD shaped his journey. For years, he struggled with feeling 'different' and battled self-doubt. But once he embraced his unique brain and focused on his strengths, his confidence skyrocketed—and so did his success."

I made a big change after hearing Michael Phelps' story. If someone like him, with all his challenges, could achieve greatness, why couldn't I? You've likely felt the weight of self-doubt too, questioning your abilities or feeling like you don't measure up. ADHD can chip away at self-esteem with constant reminders of what you "should" be doing differently. The truth is that you don't need to fix yourself to feel more confident. What you need is to see your worth and embrace your strengths.

Let's talk about how to deal with ADHD with confidence and build a strong sense of self-worth.

Why ADHD Can Hurt Your Confidence

If you have ADHD, you may be criticized for the rest of your life by teachers who didn't understand how energetic you were, by peers who thought you were forgetful, or even by yourself for not living up to societal expectations. These experiences can cause you pain and lead you to doubt your skills and value.

A well-known expert on ADHD, Dr. Russell Barkley, says, "ADHD isn't a lack of ability; it's a lack of consistency in using that ability." People naturally feel more confident when they know their skills. The first step to going from self-doubt to self-belief is to change how you see yourself.

Step 1: Figure out what you're good at.

Realizing and owning your unique skills is the first step to building confidence. ADHDers are naturally creative, empathetic, and innovative, which sets them apart.

Things you can do:

Write down all your personal and professional wins, big or small. This gives you a physical reminder of what you can do.

Seek Feedback from Others: Often, others can identify strengths that you may have missed. Ask friends or colleagues what they admire about you.

Focus on Growth Areas: Instead of fixating on what you fight with, praise areas where you've improved.

Example: Imagine reflecting on a time when your quick thinking solved a problem at work or when your imagination brought a project to life. These times are proof of your worth.

Step 2: Reframe Negative Thoughts

ADHD often comes with a harsh inner critic, but you don't have to believe every negative thought that crosses your mind. Reframing those thoughts can transform how you see yourself.

Things you can do:

Challenge Negative Narratives: When you catch yourself thinking, "I'm so disorganized," reframe it as, "I'm finding ways to get more organized every day."

Mantras: To combat self-doubt, repeat affirmations to yourself. For instance, "I am resourceful and able."

Write down your daily wins, no matter how small, in a success journal to help you feel positive about your self-image.

For example, instead of being harsh on yourself for forgetting a meeting, think about how you handled it afterward: you said sorry, rescheduled, and moved on.

Step 3: Make goals that are reasonable and doable.

Setting goals that you can reach and enjoying your progress gives you a sense of success, which boosts your confidence. People with ADHD need real wins that give them feedback right away.

Things you can do:

Start Small: Break big goals into manageable steps to avoid overwhelm.

Focus on Effort, Not Perfection: Celebrate the effort you put into tasks, even if the outcome isn't perfect.

Track Progress Visually: Use charts, apps, or planners to see how far you've come.

For instance, if you want to clean up your home, start with one box. Completing that small task gives you a dopamine boost and motivates you to tackle the next one.

Step 4: Surround Yourself with Supportive People

Your environment plays a huge role in shaping your confidence. Having individuals around you who encourage and comprehend you can significantly impact your confidence.

Things you can do:

Seek Out Your Tribe: Join ADHD support groups or communities where you can share experiences and gain inspiration.

Set Boundaries: Minimize encounters with people who criticize or damage your self-esteem.

Celebrate Together: Share your wins with supportive friends or family who truly cheer you on.

Example: Imagine joining an ADHD support group where someone says, "I struggled with that too, and here's what helped me." That sense of connection and validation is incredibly powerful.

Step 5: Learn to Recover Gracefully

You expect setbacks, but they don't define you. Being confident doesn't mean ignoring problems; it means how you deal with them.

Things you can do:

Accept Mistakes as Chances to Learn: Instead of seeing mistakes as failures, think of them as chances to get better.

Self-compassion means being kind to yourself the way you'd treat a friend.

Focus on Resilience: Think about the challenging things you've been through in the past and use them to show how strong you are.

When you miss a deadline, you think about what went wrong (for example, not managing your time well) and make a new plan (for example, setting earlier notes) to make sure you don't make the same mistake again.

Questions People Ask About Getting More Confident

"How do I deal with criticism?"''

Make an effort to distinguish between constructive criticism and unnecessary criticism. "Is this feedback useful, or is it just an opinion I can ignore?"''

"What if I'm still unsure of myself?"

Confidence is a skill, not something you are born with. Your confidence will grow as you practice recognizing wins, changing the way you think, and taking on new tasks.

How having confidence changes your life

Things change when you feel more sure of yourself. Challenges become less scary, chances become more accessible, and you begin to believe in your own strength and ability. Being confident doesn't mean you'll never have doubts; it just means you trust yourself to handle them.

Imagine that you are relaxed and ready for a meeting because you know you have useful information to share. Or you try something new, like an artistic hobby or a new task at work, without being afraid of failing. When you believe in yourself, these things can happen.

Your Plan for Boosting Your Confidence

Here's how you can begin to believe in yourself and enhance your self-esteem:

Recognize Your Strengths: Think about what you've done well and ask people who support you what they think.

Reframe Negative Thoughts: Fight self-critical stories by showing proof of your worth and encouragement.

Set goals that you can actually reach. Break up big jobs into small steps that you can easily complete.

Build a Supportive Environment: Spend time with positive and supportive people.

Recover with Grace: See failures as chances to learn and get better.

How You Can Believe in Yourself

Getting over ADHD with confidence means facing your self-doubts with strength and bravery. This section will assist you in identifying the strengths you already possess that are necessary for achieving your goals.

You are strong, smart, and have everything you need to succeed. Let's take this step together, and you'll feel fantastic about yourself.

You can put your needs first without feeling guilty with the ADHD Self-Care Plan.

She said, "I've learned that self-care means giving the world the best of you instead of what's left of you." It's a powerful message, but many of us, especially women with ADHD, find it challenging to put our own needs first.

I really felt what Beyoncé said when I heard it. How often do women put other people before themselves and forget to take care of themselves? If you have ADHD, this loop wears you down even more. Self-care can seem like an extravagance when you have a lot of things to do, ADHD symptoms to deal with, and guilt over "not doing enough." But here's the truth: putting your needs first isn't selfish; it's necessary.

There is no need to feel guilty about taking care of yourself if you have ADHD. Let these tips help you recharge, restart, and be your best.

Why is it so difficult for women with ADHD to take care of themselves?

People with ADHD often struggle with planning, scheduling, and adhering to patterns, leading them to neglect self-care. You may also feel like self-care is impossible because society expects women to take care of others.

Dr. Patricia Quinn, an expert on women and ADHD, says, "Women with ADHD often feel guilty for not living up to societal norms, which makes them ignore their own needs." To break this loop, they need to see self-care as a must instead of a nice-to-have.

Step 1: Stop negotiating self-care and see it as a must.

You need to change the way you think about self-care first. You view self-care not as a luxury or a treat, but as the foundation of your life.

Things you can do:

Challenge the Guilt: Remind yourself that taking care of yourself makes it easier for you to help other people.

Self-care doesn't have to mean a full day at the spa. One simple thing you can do is drink some water or take a five-minute break.

Say things over and over again, like, "I deserve care and attention just like everyone else."

Imagine repeatedly telling yourself, "I can't pour from an empty cup," whenever shame begins to creep in. This small shift in your mindset can significantly impact your life.

Step 2: Figure out what you need for self-care.

There is no one right way to take care of yourself, especially for people with ADHD. It's important to figure out what helps and recharges you.

Things you can do:

Think about the parts of your life that feel ignored, like your physical health, your mental health, or your ability to express yourself creatively.

Make a Self-Care Menu: Write down some small, doable things that are beneficial for you, like going for a walk, calling a friend, or writing in a book.

Balance: Take care of your body, mind, and emotions simultaneously.

For instance, you can take care of yourself by stretching for 10 minutes in the morning, engaging in activities you enjoy, and taking a moment to breathe after a busy day.

3. Make routines that work for people with ADHD.

Structure is beneficial for people with ADHD, but habits can feel overwhelming. Making self-care habits that are open and work for people with ADHD makes it easier to stick to them.

Things you can do:

Anchoring self-care to habits you already have—do things you already do to help you take care of yourself. For instance, stretch while you wait for your coffee to boil.

Set alarms or sticky notes; use these to remind yourself to take care of yourself throughout the day.

Make It Easy to See: To remember yourself, keep your self-care items, like a yoga mat or journal, in plain sight.

Say you set your phone to tell you every day to "pause and hydrate." This small action turns into a habit that is beneficial for your health as a whole.

Step Four: Learn How to Say "No"

Too many commitments can get in the way of self-care. It can be challenging to know your limits when you have ADHD, which can make you feel stressed. You can save your energy and focus on what's important by saying "no."

Things you can do:

Set limits: Turn down requests that drain you or don't fit your goals.

Use scripted phrases such as "I'd love to help, but I can't do that right now."

Make time for self-care every day and don't let anything else get in the way of it.

When a friend asks for a favor during the time you had planned to take care of yourself, you politely say no and suggest a different time. This keeps your energy safe without hurting the connection.

Step 5: Include activities that make you content

Self-care is more than just taking care of your basic needs. It also means doing things that make you fulfilled and complete.

Things you can do:

Get back into hobbies: Remember the things you loved doing in the past and make time for them now.

Play around with your creativity. Try new things, like dancing, drawing, or farming, to find out what makes you happy.

Celebrate Small Wins: No matter how simple the things that bring you joy are, let yourself know that they do.

For example, drawing in a notebook for 20 minutes may not seem like much, but it helps you feel more grounded and creative.

Questions People Often Ask About Self-Care

"How do I make time for self-care when I'm so busy?"

Begin with micro-self-care, which includes quick, one- to five-minute tasks that you can fit into your day, like taking deep breaths or drinking water. These little things do make a difference.

"What if I feel bad about giving myself time off?"

Remember that taking care of yourself isn't being selfish. You can better help the people and tasks you care about when you take care of yourself.

<u>Developing a self-care plan can significantly transform your life.</u>

Putting self-care first builds a base for growth, resiliency, and happiness. Imagine starting the day with a lot of energy, staying calm when things go wrong, and closing the day with a sense of accomplishment. Don't just take care of yourself; it affects every part of your life and makes your relationships, work, and health better overall.

Think about this: when you wake up, you stretch, drink a glass of water, and write in your notebook for five minutes. These small acts of self-care will help you feel grounded and at ease during the day.

What You Can Do to Take Care of Your ADHD

How to make a self-care plan and stick to it:

Think about self-care differently: see it as necessary, not as a treat. Affirmations can help you fight guilt.

Figure Out What You Need: Make a custom self-care plan with things that will help you feel better.

Set up routines: Connect self-care to things you already do, and use reminders to keep them.

Rules: To keep your time and energy safe, learn to say "no."

Putting joy first means making time for hobbies and activities that make you happy.

How You Want to Take Care of Yourself

The ADHD self-care plan isn't about taking on more; it's about picking what makes you feel good. Prioritizing your needs helps you stand tall for yourself and others.

You deserve love, care, and happiness. Today, let's start making a plan for how you will take care of yourself.

Getting the most out of your life with ADHD: Tried-and-true tips for the future

Emma Stone, an actor and comedian, has been open about having ADHD. She says it helps her be creative and solve problems in a unique way. She once said, "I wouldn't trade it for the world because it's part of who I am." Seeing ADHD as a source of strength instead of a problem is what changes lives.

Reframing can be very helpful, as I learned from Emma Stone's talk about her ADHD. People often teach us to view ADHD as a problem or something that requires "fixing." But if you change your mindset and learn the right tools, ADHD can become your superpower—a unique view that lets you do amazing things.

You can't get rid of problems in order to live your best ADHD life. Instead, you need to give yourself the tools to confidently face them and make a life that feels real, fulfilling, and in line with your strengths. Next, let's discuss how ADHD can help you own your future.

Why acceptance is the first step to empowerment.

One of the biggest obstacles to empowerment is resistance, such as getting angry at ADHD's problems or wishing you were "normal." But acceptance is the first step: realizing that ADHD is a part of who you are and learning to work with it, not against it.

Dr. Edward Hallowell, a renowned expert on ADHD, asserts that, with proper management, ADHD can become a strength rather than a weakness. It's all about getting to know your brain and creating methods that work for you.

Step 1: Accept that you have ADHD.

By accepting that ADHD is a part of who you are, you can feel empowered. It's just a different perspective.

Things you can do:

Educate yourself by learning more about ADHD, particularly its manifestation in women. This knowledge can help you view problems as traits rather than failures.

Celebrate Your Strengths: List the unique qualities that your ADHD brings to the table, such as your creativity, energy, and quick thinking.

Share Your Story: Being open about your ADHD can free you and help others understand and support you.

Saying to a friend, "My ADHD makes me very creative—I think of things other people would never think of" changes the story from one of a weakness to one of a strength.

Step 2: Make a plan for the future.

To live the best life with ADHD, you need to be clear on what you want. ADHD can make it challenging to stay focused on long-term goals, but creating a vision for your future helps you channel your energy.

Things you can do:

Visualize Success: Spend time imagining what a joyful life looks like for you. Where are you? What are you doing? How are you?

Set SMART goals: Break down your vision into goals that are clear, measurable, attainable, relevant, and have a due date.

Keep Your Vision Alive: To stay connected to your goals, use vision boards, write notes, or use digital prompts.

For example, if you want to start a business, set smaller goals like writing a business plan, making a website, and putting out your first product. Every move you make helps you reach your goal.

Step 3: Make systems that work well for people with ADHD.

People with ADHD need structure, but most of the time, standard methods don't work. The key to long-term success is making sure that your tactics are just right for you.

Things you can do:

Use visual tools: To help you remember what's most important, put up calendars, task boards, or sticky notes where you can see them.

Take on responsibility. To stay on track, work with a mentor, teacher, or accountability buddy.

Make decisions easier by setting up habits or default options (like planning your outfits or meals ahead of time) to avoid getting exhausted of making choices.

Instead of a long list of things to do, use a Kanban board with three sections: "To Do," "In Progress," and "Done." Seeing tasks move around on the board can keep you focused and on track.

Step 4: Follow your interests.

Instinct and new things are what drive people with ADHD. Focusing on the things and goals that truly excite you is the key to empowerment.

Things you can do:

Find Your "Hyperfocus Zones": Think about what easily grabs your attention and look for ways to work those interests into your daily life.

Say Yes to Joy: Put hobbies, projects, or job routes that play to your strengths and make you satisfied at the top of your list.

Feel free to try new things without worrying about failing. This is how you determine what makes you happy.

For example, if you love taking pictures, set aside an hour every weekend to record moments or build your resume. What you're interested in gives you energy and ideas.

Step 5: Be more resilient by being kind to yourself.

Problems will always be there, but being kind to yourself can turn failures into stepping stones. Being resilient means being kind to yourself and learning from everything that happens.

Things you can do:

Reframe Setbacks: Say to yourself, "I learned something valuable," instead of "I failed."

Focus on what's going well, even when things are bad. This is called practicing gratitude. Being thankful changes your attitude and makes you happier.

Reward Progress: To stay motivated, celebrate small wins.

If you miss a goal, think about what went wrong (for example, you might not have given yourself enough time) and change your plan (for example, you could set earlier alerts). Every step forward is a win.

Questions People Ask About Living Their Best Life With ADHD

"What if all the changes I need to make stress me out?"

Start out small. You should only work on one thing at a time, whether it's a new habit, a method, or a hobby. Over time, progress builds up.

"How can I stick to a routine when ADHD makes it hard for me to do so?"

You need to be flexible. Don't be afraid to make changes, and to stay on track, use tools like notes or accountability partners.

How being empowered changes your life

To live your best life with ADHD, you need to become the best version of yourself, not someone else. Life feels less chaotic and more purposeful when you accept that you have ADHD, set important goals, and set up routines that help you.

Picture this: you wake up excited about the day ahead and know exactly what you want to achieve. The skills and strength to solve problems give you confidence when they arise. This is the powerful ADHD life: real, satisfying, and totally yours.

Your Action Plan for Empowerment

Start living your best life with ADHD now:

Accept that you have ADHD. Focus on your skills and take pride in your story.

Vision: Imagine your ideal life and plan how to get there.

Build Custom Systems: Come up with ways to stay organized and get things done that are beneficial for people with ADHD.

Lean Into Your Passions: Set priorities for the things and goals that get you excited.

Practice being resilient by being kind to yourself and thankful when things go wrong.

Take a step into the future.

You have everything you need to live the best life with ADHD. The goal of the trip is not to be perfect but to make progress, grow, and accept the wonderful person you are.

Your future is ready for you and full of possibilities. Let's make your life one you love by taking the next step.

Chapter 5: Making Changes in Your Life

"When you prioritize yourself and embrace your unique strengths, you unlock the door to a life that feels authentic, fulfilling, and deeply empowering."

The most important things to remember from Chapter 5 are:

Putting Together Your ADHD Toolkit: To feel confident in your ability to handle life, give yourself tools that help you plan, organize, control your emotions, and take care of yourself.

Mind and Body in Harmony: Keep your mental and physical health in balance by moving, being aware, and doing self-care activities that give you energy.

Getting Over ADHD with Confidence: Boost your self-esteem by focusing on your skills, changing the way you think about negative things, and setting goals that you can reach.

The ADHD Self-Care Plan: Put your needs first without feeling guilty by doing small, regular things for yourself that are beneficial for your health and happiness.

Living Your Best ADHD Life: Utilize proven strategies to assist you, acknowledge your ADHD, and pursue your passions to infuse your life with purpose and joy.

We've talked about how to change your life with self-care, confidence, and balance. Now it's time to make a plan for success. In Chapter 6, you'll learn seven groundbreaking strategies that will help you control your ADHD, reach your goals, and make your future exciting. Let's work on your final plan for success!

CHAPTER 6: THE ADHD SUCCESS BLUEPRINT – 7 BREAKTHROUGH STRATEGIES

"The secret to lasting success isn't just working harder—it's working smarter with tools and strategies tailored to how you thrive best."

Use Mind Mapping to Your Advantage

"Have you ever sat down to plan something, only to feel like your thoughts are a tangled mess, pulling you in a dozen directions at once?"

You're not the only one who can relate to that question. For women with ADHD, it can be challenging to keep their thoughts in order. Your mind jumps from one thought to the next very quickly, which makes it challenging to concentrate or set priorities. However, what if there was a way to take that flood of ideas and shape them into a clear, doable plan?

That's where mind mapping comes in. It's a powerful tool that will help your ADHD brain work better, not worse.

How do you mind map?

Mind mapping is a way to organize your ideas visually, so you can see how they fit together. The main idea sits at the center of the page, while related ideas disperse like a web. This method works for people with ADHD because it mimics their natural way of thinking, which is nonlinear, dynamic, and full of connections.

Let's say you're planning a project, and instead of writing a list, you draw a circle in the middle of a page and label it "Project." Then, you make branches for "Tasks," "Deadlines," and "Resources" and add smaller branches with more specific information. All of a sudden, things that seemed chaotic became clear and easy to handle.

Why can mind mapping help children with ADHD?

Mind mapping is a great way to keep the brain of someone with ADHD active. Unlike rigid outlines, it allows for imagination and freedom. You can add colors, symbols, and drawings to make it visually engaging, which helps hold your attention and keeps the process fun.

Think about this: Have you ever felt stuck staring at a blank page, trying to organize your thoughts line by line? Mind mapping lifts that pressure. It encourages you to dump all your ideas onto the page in any order, connecting them later. This freedom makes starting easier and keeps your momentum going.

How to Create Your First Mind Map

Here's how you can start harnessing the power of mind mapping today:

Choose Your Central Topic: Write the main idea in the center of a blank page. For example, if you're planning a trip, write "Vacation" in the middle.

Add Branches: Draw lines outward from the center, labeling each branch with a category, like "Destinations," "Packing List," and "Budget."

Expand Each Branch: Add smaller branches with information under each group. For "Packing List," you might include "Clothes," "Toiletries," and "Electronics."

Use Visuals: Add colors, icons, or doodles to make it interesting and remembered.

Refine Your Map: Once everything is on the page, review it for clarity. Highlight goals or add dates.

An Example from Real Life

Let's say you're planning a family birthday party. Your core idea, "Birthday Party," branches into groups like "Guests," "Food," "Decorations," and "Activities." Under "Guests," you list names and RSVPs. Under "Food," you jot down meal ideas. Instead of feeling swamped, you now have a clear visual plan that captures all your thoughts.

Why Mind Mapping Empowers You

When you use mind mapping, you're not just organizing thoughts—you're accepting how your ADHD brain naturally works. Instead of fighting your nonlinear thought, you're making it into a strength. With practice, mind mapping can become your go-to tool for handling projects, fixing problems, or even brainstorming new ideas.

So, the next time you feel stuck or confused, ask yourself: "What if I let my thoughts flow freely onto the page?When you use mind mapping, the confusion in your mind turns into clarity, giving you the power to act.

FOLLOW THE TWO-MINUTE RULE.

"How often do you put off small tasks, thinking, 'I'll get to that later,' only to find them piling up and becoming overwhelming?"

It's normal to feel like you have a lot of small things to do, like emails, dishes, and quick calls. You're not the only one. Women with ADHD often put things off not because they are hard, but because they feel like they are getting in the way. It can be scary to think about starting something, no matter how small. This is where the Two-Minute Rule comes in—a easy but effective way to stop putting things off and take back control.

What Does the Two-Minute Rule Mean?

The Two-Minute Rule is simple: do something right away if it will only take two minutes or less. Don't think too much or put things off. Just do it.

Do something that might take less time than looking through social media or worrying about your to-do list: answer an email, put away a dish, or make an appointment. The Two-Minute Rule works because it clears your mind of chores you've been putting off and gives you the drive to take on bigger challenges.

Why does the two-minute rule help kids with ADHD?

People with ADHD often have trouble starting a job, which is the step where you go from thinking to doing. Even though small jobs are easy, they can feel hard to start because they don't give your brain the quick gratification or stimulation it needs.

This problem is solved by the Two-Minute Rule, which gets rid of the mental block of "later." It changes the focus of the job to something so small and quick that starting it feels less scary. Once you start a job, the dopamine rush that comes from finishing it keeps you going.

The Two-Minute Rule: How to Use It

This approach can be used in your daily life in the following ways:

Pay Attention to the Little Things: During the day, look for things that you can do without much thought, like answering a text, putting away trash, or writing down a note.

Do it right away: Don't make a mental list of the things you need to do; do them right then.

Make quick wins a habit: Do a two-minute job first thing in the morning to get things done and build energy.

Don't try to be perfect. The goal is to finish the job, not to make it perfect. A quick answer is better than none at all.

An Example from Real Life

Let's say you see a bill on the counter. Thoughts like "I'll deal with it later" keep coming back to your mind for days. You use the Two-Minute Rule to get your phone, pay the bill, and throw away the paper. The job is done. Less stress in mind.

What About Bigger Jobs?

"What if the job takes more than two minutes?" you might ask.Split it up into smaller steps. Use the Two-Minute Rule to start by organizing one box if the thought of organizing your whole closet seems too much. Often, just getting started is enough to get things moving toward more.

Why it gives you power

The Two-Minute Rule turns the ADHD trait of putting things off into a chance to do something. It makes choices easier, clears your mind, and makes you feel like you've accomplished something.

So, ask yourself, "What little thing can I do now?"You'll find that the little things don't pile up when you use the Two-Minute Rule. Instead, they shove you forward.

MAKE SCHEDULES THAT SAVE ENERGY.

"Have you ever pushed yourself to tackle a big task at the wrong time, only to feel drained and unproductive?"

You've probably seen how bad timing can ruin your day if that question rings true. Energy levels don't stay the same for women with ADHD; they rise and fall, sometimes without warning. Most of the time, traditional time management methods don't work because they assume that you can be effective at any time. What if you planned your day around your mood instead of the time? That's what energy-smart scheduling is all about—a revolutionary method that lets you use your natural rhythms to get more done without getting too tired.

Why an energy-first approach is needed for ADHD

Brains with ADHD need to be stimulated but get tired quickly when they have to do things that feel boring or too much. At different times of the day, you may feel fully tired and energized at other times. These changes aren't taken into account by traditional plans, which can be frustrating when your energy doesn't match up with the tasks you need to do.

A famous ADHD expert, Dr. Ned Hallowell, says, "Knowing your energy patterns is key to getting things done." You don't need to work harder; you just need to work better and in line with your natural flow.

Step 1: Keep an eye on your energy levels.

Knowing your own energy habits is the first thing you need to do to make an energy-smart plan.

Things you can do:

Record your Energy: Write down when you feel the most alert, enthusiastic, or tired for a week. Keep an eye out for trends.

Find Your Peaks and Slumps: Are you most alert in the morning? Do you fall asleep in the middle of the afternoon? Knowing these times helps you make good plans.

Take into account outside factors: Think about how things like food, coffee, or the quality of your sleep affect your energy.

For example, you may find that you can concentrate best between 9 a.m. and 10 a.m. it goes down between 9 and 11 a.m., then up again in the evening. Being aware of this becomes the basis of your plan.

Step 2: Put tasks with level of energy

Once you know how your energy goes up and down, you can plan your chores around those times.

Things you can do:

Plan High-Energy Tasks for Peaks: Do difficult, important tasks like problem-solving, writing, or making decisions when you are fully awake.

Avoid doing boring or low-stakes jobs when you're tired. For example, don't do emails or filing when you're tired.

Add Recharge Breaks: When you're feeling tired, plan short, planned breaks to get your energy back.

If you have the most energy in the morning, that's when you should work on your biggest job. If you want to get things done quickly, wait until the middle of the afternoon.

The third step is to make your schedule flexible.

Brains with ADHD need to be able to adapt to sudden changes in energy.

Things you can do:

Instead of setting strict hours, plan your day into chunks that you can change if your energy changes.

Make Time to Catch Up: Plan to do things you didn't get to earlier at the end of the day.

Pay attention to your body. If your energy changes without warning, don't try to be more productive. Instead, adjust.

For example, instead of making strict plans for every hour, you could block the hours of

9 a.m. to 11 a.m. for "Deep Work" and from 2 to 3 p.m. for "Admin Tasks," so you can make changes if you need to.

Questions People Often Ask About Energy-Smart Plans

"How about if my energy changes every day?""

It's okay! The goal is not to be perfect, but to be aware. Start with broad themes and make changes as needed. Being flexible is a part of the process.

"How do I get back on track when I'm feeling down?""

You can get your energy back without stopping your day by going for a short walk, stretching, drinking water, or doing a 5-minute breathing exercise.

Why this plan will work

Making plans that save energy changes the way you work. When you match your tasks with your skills, you don't have to fight against your natural rhythms. This makes each hour more productive and less draining. You'll feel more in charge and have extra energy at the end of the day.

What time of day do you feel the most energized? How can I make the most of that time?When you use energy-smart schedule, getting things done won't feel forced; it will feel normal.

USE THE THREE-STEM BASKET METHOD.

"Do you ever look at the clutter around you and feel completely paralyzed, wondering where to even start?"

You're not the only one who has ever felt stressed out by too many papers, too many things in the drawers, or too many things all over the place. Clutter isn't just a real problem for people with ADHD; it's also a mental one. It's hard to concentrate and get things done when your place is a mess, which is just like how your mind is. The good news? The 3-S Basket System is a simple way to deal with this that works well for people with ADHD. It helps you get rid of mess, arrange, and regain control without feeling too stressed.

What does the 3-S Basket System mean?

The three S's in the 3-S Basket System stand for Sort, Simplify, and Sustain. It's a way to get rid of junk that uses three real baskets or bins to make organizing easier:

Sort: Choose what to keep, throw away, or give away.

Keep only the things you really need in order and store them.

Sustain: Keep your system in good shape by checking in and making changes on a regular basis.

This method breaks down cleaning into steps that are easier for your ADHD brain to handle.

Step 1: Put your things in order

First, get three bags or boxes and write "Keep," "Toss," and "Donate" on them. Pick a small space to start, like a drawer or a room corner, and start sorting.

Things you can do:

Move each item just once: When you pick something up, you have to decide right away which box it goes in.

Important Things to Ask Yourself: Do I use this? Does it make me happy? If not, it might fit in "Donate" or "Toss."

Set a Timer: People with ADHD tend to focus too much or get sidetracked. Set an alarm to sort for 15 to 20 minutes at a time.

For instance, you work on your bathroom closet. "Donate" is for shampoo you haven't opened yet that you'll never use, and "Keep" is for everyday things.

2. Make it easier to keep what you have

Focus on the "Keep" basket after you've sorted your things. Step 3 is all about putting your things away in a way that makes sense to your ADHD brain.

Things you can do:

Use Clear Bins: Put things away in clear bins so you can quickly see what's inside.

Group Like Items: To make it easier to find things, keep things that are similar together, like pens with pens and chargers with chargers.

Put a label on everything. Labels help you remember where things go by giving you visual cues.

Your desk tools are now neatly stored in clear bins with labels. It's easier to find what you need because the pens, sticky notes, and chargers all have their own place.

Step 3: Keep the system running

The last step is to keep your group up to date. People with ADHD do best with methods that are easy to understand and use again and again, so make maintenance a part of your habit.

Things you can do:

Schedule Check-Ins: Remind yourself once a week to clean up small spaces, like your bag or the table in your kitchen.

Keep a donation bin close by so it's easy to throw away things you don't need as you find them.

Celebrate when you've stuck to your plan for a week or a month—it makes the habit stronger.

For example, you clean up your desk and put things you don't need in the donation bin every Sunday for 10 minutes. Having this habit stops the mess from coming back.

Questions People Often Ask About the 3-S Basket System

"But what if I feel too much at first?""

Start with a small area that you can handle. Do not clean your whole kitchen at once. Instead, start with one shelf or drawer. Small wins add up to big ones.

"How can I stop making more mess?""

Keep your system in good shape. Regular check-ins and a place set aside for new things help keep the mess from coming back.

Why it works for brains with ADHD

The 3-S Basket System breaks down cleaning into simple steps that are straightforward to follow. Visual order, instant progress, and built-in upkeep are all beneficial for the brains of people with ADHD because they meet their needs for structure, stimulation, and flexibility.

So, ask yourself, "What's a small area I can clean up today?"By using the 3-S Basket System, you can make your area feel calm, organized, and helpful for reaching your goals.

Use the Three C's to keep your emotions in check.

"Have you ever felt like your emotions are running the show, pulling you in directions you don't want to go and leaving you drained or frustrated?"

It's okay if this question hits home for you. One of the hardest things about having ADHD can be controlling your emotions. Keeping your feelings in check can feel like a full-time job, especially when you react quickly to something someone says or when you have trouble refocusing after a loss. The good news is that the Three C's of Emotional Regulation—Calm, Clarify, and Choose—are an easy-to-use but effective way to get back in charge of your emotions.

Why managing emotions is so important for people with ADHD

People with ADHD often feel things more strongly and have a harder time pausing before responding because of the way their brains process emotions. Even though this level of intensity can spark emotion and creativity, it can also make people act without thinking, cause confusion, or feel guilty. The Three C's give you an organized way to stop, think, and react carefully, which makes it easier to deal with emotional problems.

Step 1: Stay calm

The first "C" is about getting a sense of stability before your feelings get worse. Thoughts become less clear when you're feeling strongly emotionally charged. Techniques for calmness help you stop and give yourself time between the cause and your response.

Things you can do:

To practice deep breathing, take four deep breaths in, hold them for four counts, and then let them out for six counts. This tells your brain to take it easy.

Focus on the five senses: five things you can see, four things you can touch, three things you can hear, two things you can smell, and one thing you can taste.

Temporarily Step Away: If something is too much for you, take a short break to reset.

For example, you get an important email at work. You don't answer right away; instead, you take a deep breath and center yourself for 30 seconds. This short break stops a reactive reaction.

Step 2: Be clear

After your first response has died down, it's time to figure out how you really feel and why. People with ADHD tend to jump to conclusions, so this step helps you sort out your feelings and find the real cause.

Things you can do:

"What am I feeling right now?" is a question you can ask yourself.Putting a name on your feeling (like anger, sadness, fear, etc.) makes it less strong.

Ask Why: Think about what made you feel that way. Was it something outside, like what someone said, or something inside, like doubting yourself?

Keep a journal of your thoughts. Writing down how you feel can help you understand them and spot trends over time.

Example: After taking some time to calm down, you realized that the critical email had triggered fear of failure rather than anger. When you realize this, you can deal with the real problem instead of becoming defensive.

Step 3: Pick

The last "C" is about doing something on purpose. You act in a way that is in line with your goals and values instead of acting on impulse.

Things you can do:

Before you do anything, stop and ask yourself, "What do I want to happen in this situation?""

Use "I" statements: Be bold when you talk to others without judging them. For instance, "The feedback worries me, and I'd like to talk about it more."

Celebrate small wins: appreciating the work it takes to respond with thought instead of moving without thinking.

For example, you decide not to send a heated response to the email but instead to send a cool, professional message later that takes the feedback into account in a productive way.

Why the Three C's Help Brains with ADHD

People with ADHD can slow down their hyperactive brains by using the Three C's—Calm, Clarify, and Choose. You can regain control over your emotional reactions and lessen the overwhelm that often comes with strong feelings by planning intentional breaks and structured steps.

Ask yourself, "How can I use the Three C's when I face my next emotional challenge?"Through this method, your feelings will no longer rule you.

Use technology to help you manage your time.

"How often do you find yourself running out of time, wondering where the hours went, and wishing you had a way to stay on top of it all?"

You're not the only one who can relate to this question. Women with ADHD may find it challenging to keep track of their time. You mean well at first, but things like forgetting, distractions, or unplanned delays throw your plans off track. The beneficial news? Tech can help you regain control of your time and turn chaos into focus more than anything else.

Why ADHD and managing time don't get along

People with ADHD have trouble with executive functioning, which includes things like setting priorities, staying organized, and sticking to a plan. Time can feel vague—at times it seems to slip away, and at other times it seems to drag on forever. Technology gives you order and guidance from the outside, which helps you stay on track.

A well-known expert on ADHD, Dr. Edward Hallowell, says, "The right tools build a framework for the ADHD brain that helps it concentrate, organize, and thrive."

Step 1: Pick out the tools you need.

Apps and gadgets are not all the same. To keep from getting too stressed, start with just one or two tools that will help you with your biggest time management problems.

Things you can do:

Calendar Apps: To make plans, set notes, and make events happen again and again, use apps like Google Calendar or Apple Calendar.

Task managers: Todoist and Trello are two apps that can help you break down chores into smaller steps and see which ones are most important.

Focus Timers: Apps like Pomodoro or Forest timers set planned work periods with breaks built in.

For example, let's say you start your day by checking your digital calendar, which is linked to your to-do list app. You know what needs your care and when it needs it.

Step 2: Make tasks easier and more automated.

People with ADHD get stuck when they have too many choices or repeat small tasks. Automating those tasks can get rid of those problems and make more brain room.

Things you can do:

Set regular alarms to remind yourself of daily tasks like taking your medicine, feeding your plants, or getting ready for meetings.

Make sure your phone, laptop, and smartwatch have the same plan to stay current.

Set up routines ahead of time: To send messages or start your day off right, use smart home devices like Alexa or Google Home.

For example, at 3 p.m., your smartwatch goes off. remind you of a call that's coming up, giving you time to get ready without stress.

Step 3: Picture the time you need to stay anchored.

When someone has ADHD, time can feel vague. Tool-based time perception makes time more real and manageable.

Things you can do:

Digital Timers: Apps like Time Timer can show you the time as a shrinking circle, which will help you keep track of the minutes as they pass.

Color-Coded Schedules: To get a quick picture of your schedule, give each job or priority a different color on your calendar.

Daily calendars: If writing things down helps you remember them better, use both digital and paper calendars.

For example, if you color-code your plan, you can quickly see which blocks of time are for work, running chores, or just relaxing.

Step 4: Change your mind, but be responsible.

ADHD brains desire flexibility, but they also require accountability to maintain focus. Technology facilitates task completion.

Things you can do:

Change your plans right now: Use apps that make it simple to drag and drop chores or change your plans.

Set Progress Notifications: Apps like Habitica turn chores into games and give you rewards for finishing them on time.

Track Patterns: Toggl and other time-tracking apps can help you figure out how you spend your time and where you can improve.

For example, if you forget to do something, your app will send you a friendly reminder or let you move it to a later time without feeling negative about it.

Questions People Often Ask About Using Technology to Manage Their Time

"What if I forget to use the apps?"

Start with one app and work it into the things you already do. For instance, check your task planner every morning right after you brush your teeth.

"What if there are too many tools for me?"

Simplify your life by picking one main app or device that can do many things, like a calendar that works with your reminders.

What Technology Can Do for Brains with ADHD

Time is externalized by technology, which turns an idea into something real. It takes away the stress of remembering things, so you can concentrate on what's important.

So, ask yourself, "What's one small thing I can do today to start using technology to help me organize my time?"If you have the right tools, time won't be slipping away; it will be working for you.

MAKE A HABIT LOOP THAT IS BASED ON REWARDS.

"Have you ever started a habit with enthusiasm, only to abandon it days later because it felt too boring or hard to sustain?"

You're not the only one who has been through this. For women with ADHD, it can be hard to stick to habits. Traditional advice on how to form habits doesn't always work for people with ADHD because it doesn't take into account their need for excitement and quick satisfaction. How to solve it? A reward-based habit loop is a method for turning boring jobs into rewarding ones that are high in dopamine. This makes habits not only last but also be fun.

Why people with ADHD need rewards

People with ADHD are hard-wired to look for new things and excitement. Tasks that feel repetitive or boring can quickly lose their appeal, even if they're important. Rewards trigger the release of dopamine—the "feel-good" neurotransmitter—helping to reinforce behaviors and keep you motivated.

Dr. Russell Barkley, a renowned ADHD researcher, explains, "People with ADHD often struggle with delayed gratification. Immediate benefits are important to keeping drive and consistency." By building a habit loop that incorporates rewards, you work with your brain's natural wiring instead of fighting against it.

What Is a Reward-Based Habit Loop?

A reward-based habit loop has three parts:

Cue: A trigger that tells you to start the habit.

Routine: The action or habit you want to build.

Reward: A good result that reinforces the habit.

For ADHD, the reward is the most important aspect. It gives a sense of satisfaction that keeps you coming back for more.

Step 1: Identify Your Cue

Start by picking a clear and consistent cue for your habit. ADHD brains live on order, so the cue should be tied to something you already do daily.

Things you can do:

Connect It to Something You Already Do: For instance, start your habit right after you brush your teeth or make coffee.

Put alarms, sticky notes, or other visual cues where you'll see them to help you remember.

Set an alarm: To remember every day at the same time, use your phone or a smartwatch.

Putting your notebook on your desk will remind you to write in it every night before bed if you want to make it a routine.

Step Two: Make the routine easier.

People with ADHD often feel like their habits are too big or too complicated for them to handle. To build momentum, keep the routine simple and doable.

Things you can do:

Start Small: Take small steps to break the habit. Start by "tidying up one drawer" instead of "cleaning the house."

Focus on One Habit at a Time: Don't try to build too many habits at once; it will be too much for you.

Make It Fun: To keep things interesting, use timers, music, or a fun approach.

If working out seems too hard, commit to doing something simple like stretching or going for a short walk for five minutes.

Step 3: Give yourself a reward right away.

The prize is what keeps the habit going. For people with ADHD, short-term awards work much better than long-term ones.

Things you can do:

Use Small Treats: Give yourself a favorite snack, a short TV show, or a fun app game as a reward.

Use a habit tracker or sticker chart to keep track of your progress visually.

Do Something You Enjoy: Connect the habit to a fun activity. For example, listen to an audiobook while cleaning.

Example: After completing 10 minutes of organizing, you treat yourself to a cup of coffee or 10 minutes of scrolling your favorite social media app.

Why This Works for ADHD Brains

Building habits with a reward-based loop creates positive feedback that ADHD brains need. It turns boring jobs into chances for dopamine hits, making the habits more appealing and sustainable.

Common questions about habit loops

"What if I forget my habit?"

Revisit your cue. Make it visual, consistent, and easy to notice. Alarms or sticky notes can be very helpful.

"What if I don't want to do the habit?""

Start with the smallest form that you can make. Say to yourself, "I'll do this for two minutes." Getting started is often the hardest part, but once you do, you'll keep going.

Your plan to change habits based on rewards

Pick a Cue: Connect the habit to something you already do or use visual cues to help you remember.

Lessen the Routine: Begin small and keep it easy to handle.

Add Immediate prize: When you finish a habit, give yourself a small, important prize.

"What's a small habit I want to form, and how can I reward myself when I do it?"Building habits can be hard, but with a reward-based habit loop, it will be fun and give you power.

Seeing ADHD as a strength: Your ADHD, Your Superpower

"What if the thing that people have told you is your weakness is actually your biggest strength?""

That question changed the way I'll always think about ADHD. Feeling "less than" for years—too forgetful, too scattered, and too impulsive—was hard for me. Sense a pattern? But what if I told you that those traits, the very ones that make life feel confusing, can be turned into superpowers?

You might not believe me yet, and that's okay. Let's walk through it together.

Reframing ADHD: A New Lens

Imagine this: someone hands you a pair of glasses that let you see the world in colorful, unique ways. People with ADHD have a different way of living their lives, one that is full of creativity, energy, and possibilities.

Well-known ADHD expert Dr. Edward Hallowell says that people with ADHD have a "Ferrari brain with bicycle brakes." This means that their minds are quick, changing, and full of possibilities. Great things can be done at high speeds once you learn how to control the brakes.

Michael Phelps, Simone Biles, and Richard Branson are some of the most successful people in history. What do both of them share? ADHS. They were successful because they had ADHD, not because they had ADHD.

<u>One of your strengths is that you are very creative.</u>

Brains that have ADHD are wired to be creative. Some people think in a straight line, but your mind jumps from one idea to the next, making connections you didn't expect and seeing solutions others miss.

Some people might only think of one idea when they're thinking for a project, while others might come up with ten. You have a gift for being able to think outside the box.

The world needs new ideas, and people with ADHD are naturally creative. Accept the times when your mind wanders; that's when brilliant ideas often come to you.

<u>Strength #2: Being able to bounce back from problems</u>

If you have ADHD, you've probably had to deal with misunderstandings, abuse, and even doubts about your own abilities. But every task you've faced and gotten through has made you stronger.

Things you can do:

Think about times when you did well despite the odds.

Celebrate how those experiences have shaped your strength and determination.

Remember: Resilience isn't just about enduring; it's about growing stronger with each challenge.

<u>Strength #3: Boundless Energy and Enthusiasm</u>

ADHD gives you the ability to hyperfocus on things you're enthusiastic about, diving in with unmatched energy. While others may struggle to keep attention, you thrive when you're involved.

Example: Think about a time when you lost yourself in a project or hobby for hours, accomplishing more than you thought possible. That's your energy in action.

The key is directing that energy into activities that light you up. Find what excites you, and let your desire fuel your success.

<u>Overcoming the Myths</u>

ADHD doesn't mean you're broken or incapable—it means your brain works differently. People usually think badly of people with ADHD, but it's time to change that.

Let's Break Down the Myths:

Myth: ADHD means you can't focus.

Truth: You can focus deeply on things that truly interest you.

Myth: ADHD makes you confused.

Truth: You can build unique methods that work for you.

Each myth can be reframed as a strength when you see ADHD for what it really is: a unique and powerful way of viewing the world.

Practical Steps to Embrace Your Superpower

Here's how you can start viewing ADHD as your strength:

Focus on Your Strengths: List the things you succeed at because of your ADHD, not in spite of it.

Make Your Own Systems: Make tools and habits that work with the way your brain naturally works.

Get help from people around you. Look for teachers, friends, or groups that celebrate your skills.

What Makes You Unique

The world needs leaders with energy, different points of view, and creative answers, not everyone who thinks the same way. The way your ADHD brain is wired means it can make a big difference.

If you ever feel stressed or angry, stop and ask yourself, "How can I turn this challenge into an opportunity?""

In conclusion, Accepting your ADHD Journey

Before you put this book down, I want you to think about the amazing trip you've been on. Every chapter has helped me become more confident, true to myself, and happy in my life, where ADHD isn't a problem but a strength.

In Chapter 1, you learned how to see your ADHD as a gift. In Chapter 6, you learned how to make energy-smart plans and form habits that will last. Now you have the tools and knowledge to go through life with confidence and clarity. This is more than just a set of tools; it's a plan for turning your problems into chances and your hopes into reality.

This is what I want you to take away:

Your ADHD is a strength because it makes you passionate, creative, and strong. Take pride in the way your mind works.

Small Changes Lead to Big Wins: Every small step you take is a step toward growth, whether it's the Two-Minute Rule or the Three C's of Emotional Regulation.

Self-Care Isn't Selfish: Putting your mental and physical health first lets you give your all to others and yourself.

You Are Not Alone: The tips, tools, and stories in this article are meant to remember you that other people are going through the same thing you are. Having a group and being connected makes you stronger.

You have everything you need to do well. You have the power inside you and the tools in your hands. Now is the time to accept your ADHD, live your true life, and take big steps toward the life you've always dreamed of.

You're already enough. You can't be stopped. Now shine out there.

THANK-YOU NOTES.

This book, like all books, wasn't written by one person. I want to show my sincere appreciation to those who helped make this trip possible:

To the people who read this book: You are its heart and soul. I'm so impressed by how brave you are to want to grow and change. Thanks for putting your faith in me to lead you on this trip.

To everyone with ADHD: Your stories, ideas, and strength have shaped every word on these pages. I'm proud to be a part of a group that is so active and supportive.

Thank you to my family and friends for always being there for me, being patient, and believing in my mission. At every step of this process, your support has been there for me.

Thanks to Dr. Edward Hallowell, Dr. Russell Barkley, Dr. Patricia Quinn, and many others who have done groundbreaking study and pushed for ADHD to be seen as a strength, we can now understand and accept it.

To the hidden heroes: my editor, proofreaders, and design team—your skills and hard work have made this book come to life. Thanks for making it great.

To everyone reading this, I want to say thanks for being a part of this story. This is not the end of your trip; it is just the start. People with ADHD and I are working together to change the story and show the world what's possible.

With thanks and love,

Rebecca Elwin

Resources

- https://www.additudemag.com/adhd-personal-stories-real-life-people-living-with-adhd/
- https://www.verywellmind.com/tips-for-women-with-adhd-4062682
- https://www.additudemag.com/adhd-success-stories-women-with-add/
- https://www.simplypsychology.org/tips-for-managing-adhd-as-a-woman.html
- https://www.additudemag.com/women-leaders-with-adhd/
- https://www.additudemag.com/dealing-with-adhd-80-coping-strategies/
- https://neurolaunch.com/adhd-stories/
- https://www.merakilane.com/adhd-in-women-17-tips-for-managing-adult-adhd/
- https://adhdonline.com/articles/7-famous-females-thriving-with-adhd/
- https://www.theminiadhdcoach.com/adhd-awareness/adhd-in-women
- https://www.superwomansociety.org/post/6-inspiring-women-with-adhd-who-are-redefining-success
- https://www.additudemag.com/adhd-in-women-tips-for-managing-home-and-life/
- https://www.iadhd.org/personal-stories
- https://www.additudemag.com/wellbeing-strategies-adhd-women/
- https://www.adhdlifesimplified.com/blog/6-famous-women-thriving-with-adhd-after-diagnosis
- https://conquermyadhd.com/adhd-for-woman/
- https://www.healthywomen.org/real-women-real-stories/adult-with-adhd
- https://sensa.health/blog/adhd-women/
- https://www.healthywomen.org/real-women-real-stories/i-was-diagnosed-with-adult-adhd-heres-what-i-learned
- https://www.thecounselingpalette.com/post/womenwithadhd

FREE GIFT

As a way of saying thanks for your purchase, I'm offering the book Shadow Work Journal: A Journey of Self-Discovery for FREE to my readers.

To get instant access just go to:

Inside the book, you will discover:

- How to uncover hidden aspects of yourself through guided prompts

- Techniques for integrating your shadow self into your conscious life

- Exercises to foster emotional growth and self-awareness

- Practical tips for creating a balanced and fulfilling life

If you want to embark on a journey of self-discovery and transformation, make sure to grab the free book.